CMMI
Implementation Guide

A Practitioner's Perspective

Vishnuvarthanan Moorthy

ISBN: **1491072873**
ISBN-13: **978-1491072875**

DEDICATION

To the Supreme Power!

He Creates, He Maintains, He Destroys and He
Authors!

CONTENTS

Preface   9

1   Introduction to CMMI   Pg 11

2   Initiating CMMI Implementation   Pg 20

2.1   Do I need CMMI   Pg 20

2.2   Establish Internal Commitment   Pg 21

2.3   Choosing the Right Constellation   Pg 23

2.4   Engaging Service Provider   Pg 25

3   Planning CMMI Implementation   Pg 28

3.1   Gap Analysis   Pg 28

3.2   Steering Committee   Pg 31

3.3   Software Engineering Process Group   Pg 32

3.4   Process Quality Assurance Group   Pg 33

3.5   Schedule your CMMI Program   Pg 34

3.6   Estimate for CMMI Program   Pg 37

3.7   Change Management   Pg 40

4   Executing CMMI Implementation   Pg 43

4.1   Process Definition   Pg 43

4.2   Quality Management System   Pg 47

4.3   Roles and Responsibilities   Pg 50

4.4   Training in CMMI Program   Pg 51

4.5   Handholding Period   Pg 53

4.6	Key Activities in CMMI Implementation	Pg 54
4.6.1	Selection of Projects/Units	Pg 54
4.6.2	Compliance Checks	Pg 56
4.6.3	Consulting Activities	Pg 57
4.6.4	Process QA Group Activities	Pg 61
4.6.5	Spot Checks	Pg 62
4.6.4	Sources for Process Improvements	Pg 65
4.6.7	Repositories Set Up	Pg 66
4.7	CMMI Development Implementation	Pg 67
4.8	CMMI Services Implementation	Pg 76
4.9	Generic Goals and Practices	Pg 87
5	Appraising CMMI Implementation	Pg 92
5.1	Appraisal Scope Discussion	Pg 93
5.2	Appraisal Team Member Selection	Pg 95
5.3	Appraisal Plan	Pg 97
5.4	Readiness Review	Pg 97
5.5	Preparation for Scampi A	Pg 97
5.6	Scampi A onsite Activity	Pg 98
6	Sustaining CMMI Implementation	Pg 100
7	CMMI High Maturity Implementation	Pg 102
7.1	Organizational Process Performance	Pg 106
7.2	Quantitative Project/Work Management	Pg 115
7.3	Causal Analysis and Resolution	Pg 119

7.4   Organizational Performance Management   Pg 120

8   Agile with CMMI and Alternate Practices   Pg 125

8.1   Agile with CMMI   Pg 125

8.2   Alternate Practices   Pg 134

9   References   Pg 136

PREFACE

This CMMI Implementation Guide is a reference book for anyone interested in implementing CMMI in their organization. The purpose of this book is, to provide insight in to CMMI Implementation phases and best practices to be followed in this journey. Most of us agree, that CMMI is more a De facto model that IT Industry follows and other industries also has shown lot of interest in adopting this model. The day to day popularity and its adoption rate is on the surge for CMMI. In this scenario, this book will help the new organizations and implementers, on how to approach CMMI Implementation practically in their organization. This book is not a replacement to the Model or to the resources which CMMI Institute Publishes. This is only an additional resource which user can benefit from.

CMMI Institute holds the complete authority and rights to CMMI model and all the components within the framework. This book is prepared based on the experience of a practitioner on implementing the model in various organizations. The Author has worked in multiple roles in CMMI Implementation and has global exposure in implementing the model. We reiterate that for all the model related details and updates, please visit CMMI Institute website and contact CMMI Institute team for any clarifications.

This book is intent to give you guidance on how to approach CMMI Implementation in your organization from initiation, planning, execution, appraisal and sustenance. This book gives various practical approaches followed by organizations as typical examples. Implementation of CMMI is not an activity for marketing and bidding, it's more than that, its strengthening of your product development & Service delivery models to achieve your business results. Considering this you would want CMMI Implementation to bring in the real cultural change and value to your business. This book provides you information which is useful for deciding, planning and implementing CMMI in Successful way.

Be clear, there are many ways to implement CMMI and its practices.

Having a better consultant or Engaging a CMMI Institute Partner in your Journey is always helpful in removing the barriers at right time, however in this book we are giving the details, which one should be aware of in this journey to better utilize the resources and control the program.

This book is suggested for senior management people, process quality assurance people, delivery people and anyone interested to know about CMMI Implementation. Understanding on the topics given in this book will help them to strategize for successful CMMI Implementation.

INTRODUCTION TO CMMI

CMMI (Capability Maturity Model Integration) is a Process Improvement Model, which has collection of Industry best practices to implement in Organizations to achieve process capability and maturity. CMMI is a proven approach to achieve better performance results. CMMI is more of a framework which contains the model, trainings and appraisal components which helps an organization to implement the model in successful way to get benefit out of it. CMMI over the years has shown lot of success considering organizations are getting dramatic improvements in effectiveness, efficiency and quality.

Software Engineering Institute in Carnegie Melon University has developed this model initially. The CMMI Model Evolution is given below,

Year	Model Development
1987	Initial Framework
1990	CMMv1.0
1993	CMMv1.1
1998	CMMv2.0
2000	CMMIv1.0

2002	CMMIv1.1
2006	CMMIv1.2
2010	CMMIv1.3

*Source – CMMI Institute Site

In the year 2012 -2013 the CMMI Model and related components have been transitioned to the newly formed CMMI Institute for better management and results. For further details, please refer CMMI Institute site and/or contact Customer relations of CMMI Institute.

The current version of CMMI is Version 1.3 and it got released in year 2010 and related appraisal version SCAMPI v1.3 also available. The model can be downloaded for free in CMMI Institute site. CMMI has three different Constellations in its product suite. As definition "a constellation is subset of CMMI product suite relevant to improvement in a particular area of interest". The constellations are CMMI for Development, CMMI for Services and CMMI for Acquisition.

CMMI for Development - Addresses guidance on product/System development/Engineering

CMMI for Services - Addresses guidance on delivering services to internal and external entities

CMMI for Acquisition – Addresses supply chain management, acquisition and outsourcing processes in government and in Industry.

These CMMI Constellations are having set of Process Areas designed to achieve results in that area. However there are 16 common process areas between all the three models. The other process areas are specific to that constellation. In this book, we are limiting ourselves with CMMI Dev (CMMI for Development) and CMMI SVC (CMMI for Services). In CMMI Dev we have 6 specific Process Areas and in CMMI SVC we have 7+1 Specific Process Areas. The CMMI Dev consists in total 22 Process Areas and CMMI Svc consists in total 23(+ Service System Development) Process Areas.

Process Area is a cluster of related practices to achieve certain results. Process Areas are organized in terms of Goals and each Goal consists of set of practices, which would help to achieve the goals. An Example: Configuration related practices to be performed in product development or in Service Delivery are collected and established under one process area called "Configuration Management". Risk identification and handling practices are established under "Risk Management" process area.

CMMI consists of two representations, Staged Representation and Continuous Representation. Staged Representation is adopted by most of the organizations as its giving them guidance and benchmarking with other Organizations, Whereas continuous representation is adopted by Organizations which are clear in their area of improvement and are comfortable with the practices in all other areas (or comfortable with the level of performance).In Staged Representation, Organization's Maturity level is provided with 5 different process maturities. In Continuous Representation, Each process Areas' capability levels are presented with 6 levels. A representation in CMMI is analogous to a view into a dataset provided by a database. Both representations provide ways of implementing process improvement to achieve business goals. Both representations provide the same technical content, but organized into different ways.

In this guide, we will concentrate on the Staged Representation based on Maturity Level. A Maturity Level is a well-defined evolutionary plateau on the path to becoming a mature organization. Each level provides foundation to the next Maturity level. Each Maturity level Consists of set of process areas to be implemented. There are five maturity levels in CMMI Staged representation.

Maturity Level	Definition	Characteristic
Level 1	Initial	Poor Control & Heroism
Level 2	Managed	Project Processes & Reactive

Level 3	Defined	Organization Process & Proactive
Level 4	Quantitatively Managed	Predictable and controlled Process
Level 5	Optimizing	Process Improvement & Innovation

*source – CMMI Model

Each Process Area consists of Goals. Goals are further aligned with related practices and a goal indicates combined achievement of practices under it. There are two types of Goals,

- Specific Goals: Implementation Specific to that Area of Interest is the target

- Generic Goals: Institutionalization of the process area is the target

Each Goal consists of set of Practices to be performed. A Practice indicates the related tasks to be performed. There are two types of practices,

- Specific practices: Specific and unique itself. Information differs from level to level

- Generic practices: Common practices across all process areas with a similar grouping

In addition to this there are sub practices, notes and sample work products. They help us to understand the intent of the model components and implement it better.

Further details on architecture and understanding on Goals and practices, please refer to the CMMI model (The model is a registered copyrighted product of CMMI Institute).

Maturity Level	CMMI Dev Process Areas	CMMI Svc Process Areas
Level 2	Requirements Management	Requirements Management
	Project Planning	Work Planning
	Project Monitoring and Control	Work Monitoring and Control
	Supplier Agreement Management	Supplier Agreement Management
	Configuration Management	Configuration Management
	Measurement and Analysis	Measurement and Analysis
	Product and Process Quality Assurance	Product and Process Quality Assurance
	------------	Service Delivery
Level 3	Requirements Development	Strategic Service Management
	Technical Solution	Incident Resolution and Prevention
	Product Integration	Service Transition
	Verification	Service Continuity
	Validation	Capacity and Availability Management
	Integrated Project Management	Integrated Work Management

	Risk Management	Risk Management
	Decision Analysis and resolution	Decision Analysis and resolution
	Organizational Training	Organizational Training
	Organizational Process Definition	Organizational Process Definition
	Organizational Process Focus	Organizational Process Focus
	------------	Service System Development (Add)
Level 4	Quantitative Project Management	Quantitative Work Management
	Organizational Process Performance	Organizational Process Performance
Level 5	Organizational Performance Management	Organizational Performance Management
	Causal Analysis and Resolution	Causal Analysis and Resolution

*Add – Additional Process Area: Applicability decided by Need of the Organization

CMMI – Known Benefits:

- Improvements in Project/Work performance Results

- Achievement of Business Objectives

- Delivery and Service Systems are streamlined

- Quality Improvement in service and product

- Lesser customer complaints

- Improved employee morale

- Standardized delivery approach in business

- Understand the Strength and Weakness in process and plan improvements

- Better process – product relationship achievement

- Predictability and continual improvements helps business growth

- Better Engineering and Service Processes

- Helps in Adopting Newer Technologies in Quick time

- Scaling up of process to new methodologies is comparatively easier

- Better Project Management and Control in the Organization.

Please visit CMMI Institute site for further details and for reports on Quantitative gains.

Beyond all this, we have to acknowledge the fact that CMMI from Information Technology Industry perspective is a De facto Model and it has ensured that more and more organizations has standard engineering process development practices, there by contributed to the industry and to customers. In last 15 years, as the industry and new technology practices has grown, CMMIs contribution is vital to the Industry. We have to thank SEI and CMMI Institute for ensuring this model is up to date and paved way for us to standardize and improve our delivery practices. CMMI is instrumental in bringing Process Based Delivery Approach, Stable quality management system, bringing Process Quality Assurance practices more explicit, Clarity in software Engineering Concepts and establishing Strong Process Working Groups in the Industry. Having said that, CMMI is beyond software and Systems, however in this guide we limit only to the IT Industry.

Few Key Success Factors for its worldwide adoption:

- The users can contribute and raise change requests to customer relations

- Users of the model can ask clarifications and they are supported well by CMMI Institute

- The New changes are discussed and piloted in many cases

- New improvements are always welcome with CMMI Institute

- The Model and related sources are free and users can download

- Apart from Appraisal and official Training there is no mandated cost involved

- The Proven results made it as a model widely adopted across the globe

- CMMI Partners are available worldwide and getting services are easier

- User groups in Yahoo, LinkedIn and other social sites help in people to understand and clarify doubts

- Systematic working and bringing in changes to help users by the CMMI Institute and all its certified personnel is strength.

- The Quality of the results are monitored and relevant policy updates are given by CMMI Institute to ensure that Users get good experience in Implementing the model and performing appraisals

- The case studies, presentations, webinars on different topics performed by CMMI Institute to ensure that all kind of industries get relevant update.

- SEIR repository provides enormous amount of user contributed materials, which helps every organization and its employees to get better understanding and implementation of the model.

- CMMI Institute and associated members/partners work on different areas of interest and share updates on them to the community. Most of them are free articles. Example: Agile and CMMI, in this area lot of effort spent by community members and today we can say, we are no longer with many ambiguities in adopting CMMI and Agile together.

- Combined Constellation implementations and combined appraisals has also become reality and many of the organizations are interested considering their business model.

- CMMI Institute SEPG meetings which happens once in every 6 month, brings in lot new ideas and process approaches, which is critical for the evolving trends in the Industry. In short they work on maintaining the Model up to date.

INITIATING CMMI IMPLEMENTATION

Do I need CMMI?

The first step in CMMI Implementation is to understand what you want to achieve in your product development or service delivery. For that you have to be clear with your current business model and the role of processes in your business. There can be no business without any process in this world. However the balance between process, technology and people could vary from one to another. Hence it's important to understand what is the role of process in your business and by improving its maturity, what is the kind of result you expect with your business to be understood. This we can say, "Do I need CMMI?" CMMI may not be a solution for all the problems you have and just because someone has told, you may not start your implementation.

You are expected to have the clear understanding of current Business and related processes, in addition to that, now you are expected to set your objectives for CMMI Implementation. We can look at any similar organizations which has implemented the model and how the results have paid for them. With little more research on your own and with CMMI Institute site and relevant reports, you can have an idea about how CMMI Implementation can help in your business and in delivery.

When we say understand your business, it means

- What are the different products or services your organization offer

- How many divisions and units are there

- Do all of them produce same or similar products/services

- Are all of them produce same business benefit or which of them are key for me to succeed in business

- Are you already in the optimum level or there is scope for improvement

- Which part of the business to improve or Business process to improve

- What is the cycle time of my services or products

- Do you produce part of product/service or complete product/service

- Are you interacting with client directly or with your own resources (onsite teams)

- What is the current resource competency I have

- What is the level of Infrastructure you have

- Whether you are clients are expecting you to perform with certain maturity in some processes

The Understanding on these questions will help you to think more on what you are going to gain by implementing CMMI. Also it will tell, do you really inclined to implement CMMI or its just for Attracting clients or for bidding purpose, you want to get some maturity level. Because when we are not aware of our business model and where exactly we feel CMMI Implementation will benefit us in our business, then we have more chances of not getting the real benefits of CMMI.

Establish Internal Commitment:

Discuss within management about what CMMI is, and what kind of benefits you are expecting from implementing the model in your organization. Be specific on the results and be clear that questions may come on the following, Why CMMI model and why not others, what benefit it will give, how can we apply in our business, etc. The reality is almost 90% of the organizations might have the same questions; however they have implemented the model and getting benefits today. It's pretty normal that everyone thinks that their business is unique, their project is unique and they are unique. However most of them can be categorized in countable number of groups and many of them has similar characteristics, so CMMI is no difference to it. Set clear expectations with people on what level of involvement you expect and where the changes are likely to come. Many times, fear of change and modification of system will make people resist the Implementation. Hence clarity on what is expected, what might change, what benefit it will bring, motivating them to be part of change and making them own the changes will help to great extent. Involve the Heads of all the functions in your discussion, so that everyone feels part of the initiative.

Give time to people to think and come back on the CMMI Initiative. Let the questions come on the initiative and anything on the model, it's better to answer it through an Executive Session on CMMI. The Session could be typically for a day, so that better clarity and understanding all the senior management people achieve. This could help you in removing the anxiety from the stakeholders.

Initial discussion with Subject Matter Expert:

Once all the stakeholders are in alignment you can go ahead and have discussion with the CMMI Subject Matter Expert (SME). You may find one internally in your organization or you may contact any CMMI Partners in your region, who are providing the Consulting and Appraisal services. You can check the list of CMMI Partners and their services through CMMI Institute site. A discussion with Subject Matter Expert should be on the following,

- Current Version and Status of CMMI Model

22

- What are the different steps involved in Implementation

- What phases and approach they generally suggest to the organization

- Data/Experience related to Similar Cases of Implementation

- Check the ROI that Other Organizations have achieved

- What the different Objectives that Organization like yours can aim to achieve

- What are the different requirements on Human, Infrastructure, training requirements

- What is the right Constellation according to the SME for your business

- Have them describe the overall expectation from the Organization

- Collect the Contact points and relevant references for them (for external Service Providers)

- It may be too early, however you can check with them the timeline typically it takes to implement CMMI Model on an Organization like yours and the maturity level you should target.

CMMI Institute always keeps their database up to date on their Partners; hence selecting a Service Provider from there is not a difficult choice. At the same time, there are many other renowned organizations also providing CMMI Consulting services. You have the option of selecting among many, but for Appraisal and formal training services from CMMI Institute, it shall be done through CMMI Partners only with the CMMI Certified Individuals. However for consulting or SME services there is no such restriction.

Choosing the right Constellation for you:

As we already discussed that you have worked on the basics of your business and what you expect from CMMI Implementation. However when it comes to selection of CMMI Constellations for your business, you may end up with question, which one to choose. It can be decided on few factors,

- Business Model in the Organization

- Typical Cycle Time to deliver your Product or Services

- Volume of work in Service Delivery and Product Delivery

- Business Income ratio between Service Delivery and Product Delivery

- Complexity involved in Product Development

- Areas where you need Improvement

- Type of Activities Performed

There could be other factors which also can influence. However when you find they are smaller cycle times in which you have to deliver your product or services and less intensive engineering needs, then its recommended to go for CMMI Services. However if you are involved equally on development of product and in Services (Maintenance/migration/testing/etc) then you can go for combined CMMI Dev and CMMI Svc Constellations to have the best from both. In case if you have lot of medium (3 to 9 month) and Longer Projects (> 9 months) and need good Engineering Practices to strengthen your product, you can select CMMI Dev model.

Be clear CMMI Svc doesn't mean there are no engineering practices; it has Service System Development process area to support your needs. However you have to decide based on what level of complexity, your products have.

Fix your Goal on the Program:

The following aspects you have to be clear before engaging in to the planning part of CMMI Implementation in your organization.

- Clear description on your business needs on CMMI Implementation

- Performance Goals target for your business

- Tools and Technology Improvements or positioning

- Prioritization of process based delivery and Services

- Competency level of Employees and target improvements

- Possible Effort and Availability requirements of Management Team

- Possible effort needs from SME and Process Quality Assurance people

- Return on Investment expected from the program (direct and in-direct)

Once you have made up your mind on the above given points then it's time for you to engage Service Provider.

Engaging CMMI Institute Partner or Service Provider:

As explained earlier, you would definitely need a CMMI Institute Partner for performing a) CMMI Official Trainings b) Appraisal Services. For CMMI Consulting Activities, you can engage any Subject Matter Expert from your own organization or from other service provider or through a CMMI Institute Partner. If Appraisal is in your plan and you want to achieve a Maturity Level rating, then it's important that you understand that you need a CMMI Institute certified Lead Appraiser for performing your appraisal. A Lead Appraiser services can be availed through the CMMI Institute Partner. Engaging Lead Appraiser early in your implementation helps you to be in alignment with his expectations and to ensure his availability for your program.

The following points you need to consider before engaging any of them:

a) Consider the overall experience of the Lead Appraiser and relevant experience in the area of working

b) Interact with them to see how they are able to pick up your business model and services

c) Check their credibility in the market

d) Cost of the Appraisal services (include Logistics cost)

e) Past experiences and similar organization appraisals performed by them

f) Collect References for their work

g) Get their view on your CMMI Implementation program

h) Understand their schedule and how busy they are. (There is a cap of 12 appraisal per year/ per LA, hence check whether they are available for you)

i) Sponsor of CMMI Program has to interact with the Lead Appraiser, before engaging them

j) Check your comfort level with Lead Appraiser. Sometimes few are comfortable with aggressive type of Individual and some are comfortable with soft spoken, friendly Lead Appraiser.

k) Check what are all the different product modules (Trainings, Appraisals) he is certified for, that can reduce your interaction with multiple Certified Individuals.

l) Check on the best possible review schedule and Appraisal schedule they suggest to you.

Be clear a Lead Appraiser who is going to perform your appraisal, cant' be a consultant for you. Similarly if you have your own Lead Appraiser, then he/she can't be from the same Organizational Unit (the Organizational unit which is within the scope of Appraisal).

Most of the points given here holds true for selecting a Consultant, however for that you don't need a CMMI Institute Partner. CMMI Institute doesn't mandate consulting activities under any case and Implementation of the model, can be completely done by in house or with any known service provider. The fact is CMMI Institute monitors the conflict of Interest that same registered organization shall not consult and perform appraisals. Under any case, CMMI Institute collects declarations from Partners and from Individuals in different times.

Common Reasons for Ineffective CMMI Implementation:

Before you start the complete planning of your CMMI Implementation program, be aware of the Common reasons which could make your CMMI Implementation in-effective.

- Lack of business alignment

- Lack of management participation

- CMMI Implementation Program for *"customer demand'*

- Lack of project management competency

- Not considering as *"Organizational Program"*

- Resistance to change

- Lack of belief in process improvement

- Interpretation challenges

- Lack of clarity in ROI

- Lack of resources

- Separation of Finance metric from Process metric

- Failure to understand the significance of *"Product and Process relationship"*

PLANNING CMMI IMPLEMENTATION

The first step recommended is to understand your current product and/or service delivery practices and its gap with CMMI Constellations which you are targeting. This would help you to plan your activities, timelines, estimation on resources, establishing/modifying working functions and strategize for effective implementation of CMMI. Hence a Gap Analysis is the recommended first step in Planning. Gap Analysis can be performed by internal Subject Matter Expert (SME) or with external one. Basically you do this exercise to understand the gaps in your defined processes (if you have one) and with Practices followed in Service/product delivery. Also a good understanding on the Organizational dynamics and gaps identified there would be values add for you.

Gap Analysis:

Planning a Gap Analysis, involves the service/delivery centers in different places, type of delivery models, type of business, duration of projects/programs, etc Based on these factors identify set of projects/program/applications which you want to take as sample for your Gap Analysis. Performing Gap Analysis involves a) Artifact Study and b) Interview/Discussion with practitioners. A detailed Gap Study will reduce lot of ambiguities and estimation errors in the subsequent stages of the program. Fix time with your practitioners and perform gap analysis with CMMI constellation that has been chosen. Check the relevant artifacts given by them to understand the delivery model and the current maturity.

Prepare a draft report in terms of Process Definition gaps and Process Implementation gaps for each of the Process Area. With certain number allocation for compliance with practices, you can also give an indicative value for Compliance with the model. Though it's inaccurate, it definitely helps organizations to visualize the compliance and to understand how much gap they have. A Gap Analysis report is the basis for planning and to work on removing the weaknesses, hence a detailed report is required. The Draft report has to be discussed with the management and final report to be prepared. Consensus with your management team ensures accuracy is established in the report. A good Gap Analysis report will also have significant weaknesses identified and provides key recommendations for next level planning. The Gap Analysis should also consider the relevant tools available and used in your organization. Any existing standards compliance by your organization to be considered in the gap analysis, as this would help in evaluating the process understanding and Management system maturity.

Strategize and Plan your CMMI Program:

We call it as a program here, considering that your entire organization is involved in it and it brings cultural change in the organization and beyond that you may need to run lot of smaller projects within this CMMI Implementation program to make it effective and bring desired results for you. Having said that, it also depends on how big is your organizational Unit, for which you are targeting the CMMI Implementation. Now based on the Gap Analysis, Understand the following,

a) Process Definition Gaps to be filled

b) Delivery and Service practices where improvement is needed

c) Roles and responsibilities update required

d) Quality Management System Establishment (set of process, technology and role which is set up to achieve desired results in delivery)

e) Type of Projects/Works targeted under CMMI Implementation

f) Organization structure update

g) Training Needs in your organization

h) Where maximum benefit can be realized with CMMI Implementation

i) Compliance Program and Metrics culture status update

Based on these factors and understanding your organization's dynamics and change management ease, derive your Goals on the following,

• CMMI Constellation to be Implemented

• Representation to be used

• Target Maturity Level

• Timeline Target for achieving the desired Maturity Level

• Performance Goals for the Program

• Business Performance Expected after CMMI Implementation

• Coverage of Business Units/Delivery Centers within scope of Implementation

Be clear your timeline has to be little aggressive than what you can achieve. Relaxed timelines and Very Aggressive timelines both can affect quality of implementation. Maturity Level consideration wise, you can select anything between Level 2 to level 5 as your target. However you can't skip any Maturity Level, it means you need to implement all the Process Areas belonging to the Lower Maturity Level, along with the one which you are targeting. Also understand it's more of a good practice, that before you target Higher Maturity levels like ML4 and

ML5, its better that you achieve ML3. A Maturity Level is not a rank, but it's the actual process maturity status in organization. Unless you perform at certain level consistently, it would be difficult for you to understand what makes your organization perform at that maturity, and after knowing that and securing your strengths, you can move to the next Maturity Level. Else you might be working with unstable system and trying to simulate Maturity only on certain accounts, which could result in negative results and poor employee morale.

Discuss with your SME/CMMI Institute Partner:

Discuss the timelines, scope of implementation, Maturity Level targeting with your CMMI SME (Subject Matter Expert)/ CMMI Institute Partner and ensure that all of you are in alignment and see the possibilities of making the program success. Understand the additional points which you need to take care in this implementation program. You can't have very different plans from your service provider that will not help to achieve your results. Be open and seek support as required. Do not consider CMMI Implementation as Process definition and Audit, such thinking will definitely cost your organization badly.

Planning the Elements in Implementation:

Organization Structure:

If you don't have any existing process standard or model implementation in your organization, than you may need few new functions in your organization. Typically for CMMI Implementation you may need,

Steering Committee:

Steering Committee is formed to ensure that program runs smoothly and any barrier is removed without delay. The Steering committee consists of senior management, head of all relevant functions and CMMI program manager. If sponsor participates in the steering committee, then it will be very effective.

- They decide on business needs and process needs

- They Communicates to Organization

- They decide on CMMI program and its implementation

- Reviews progress periodically

- They remove the barriers

- They monitor the overall progress of the program

CMMI Program Manager:

This person is responsible for monitoring and controlling the CMMI program in your organization. The person can be dedicated or partially allocated, though dedicated model always works better.

- Prepares the plan for CMMI Program

- Monitors and controls the program

- Manages the projects and stakeholders

- Reports to Steering Committee

- Participates in SEPG, Steering Committee and CMMI progress meetings

- Mobilizes the resources effectively to achieve target

- Risk management is handled and timely escalations are performed

Software Engineering Process Group (SEPG):

The group consists of Subject Matter Experts from various engineering and management areas and Process quality assurance members. Few of the SME's can be permanent members and few can work on need basis (depending on how often their process is discussed). Typically each SME is identified with relevant processes in mind. The Process Quality Assurance Members who are contributing in process definition and who are performing facilitation & audits shall represent. This helps in getting real issues from the ground and discusses with SME and put it in presentable process format.

- SEPG is responsible for Process Focus and alignment with business objectives

- SEPG ensures that relevant processes are defined to support the delivery

- SEPG ensures that process assets are created and maintained

- SEPG makes deployment and process action plans

- Process revision and maintenance is taken care by them

- Process tailoring and relevant analysis is performed

- Process Improvements achievement and sources maintenance

- SEPG is responsible for process appraisals

Practically most of the organizations, hands over the Organizational Process Focus and Organizational Process Definition process areas to SEPG. If you aim for ML4 and ML5, then Organizational Performance Management may be handled by them.

Process Quality Assurance Group:

This group consists of people who has competency on process quality assurance. Typically it includes people who can understand the process architecture, its application and improvement needs. Process compliance activities like QA reviews and Process compliance audits are performed by them. Independency and objectivity should be maintained on forming this group.

- Project facilitation and hand holding on Process implementation

- Process training performed by them

- Product Quality Assurance review performed

- Process Compliance Audits are performed

- Project level metrics analysis support

- Tailoring of processes are supported

- Interact with SEPG, project teams and metrics team to provide relevant updates

- Some organizations use them for Risk Assessment or other security compliance standards implementation.

The members in this team can be full time or part time. However full time people bring in lot of value addition, considering that they work on specific areas, bring objectivity, no conflict of interest, etc.

Metrics Analyst Group:

This group consists of people who have understanding on project management, statistics and process control. Their ability to understand the data and process is important to do further analysis. The project management understanding is more of logical understanding of project's phases and actual condition. The analysis and reporting shall be meaningful for the project and organization to use it for informed decision making. This group may not exist in all organizations and may be in High Maturity organizations (ML4 and ML5), and some organizations combines their project management office with metrics group.

Schedule your CMMI Program:

You can make a realistic schedule based on estimation of effort and activities involved in the program. Most often people prefer to work back from the final target. Hence your schedule of activities has to fit within that target, and your estimation is based on what you need to achieve within the time limit. However many a times organizations understand, that it's a program for maturity and not for report card, so they revise their time limit. On any case, have a high level plan first to check, how good is the available time for you to achieve the target. Remember it's not about a project, it's about an organization which consists of multiple functions and many people, so it's not that easy to fit any date and activity to get consensus, there is in fact lot more to think.

The following activities to be considered on making your schedule for CMMI implementation for ML2 and ML3,

Activities	Start Date	End Date	Remarks
Gap Analysis and Strategizing			
CMMI Project Kick-off			
Steering Committee and SEPG formation			
Lead Appraiser/CMMI Partner selection			
Process Definition and CMMI Mapping			
CMMI Overview Training for key stakeholders			
Process Training by role in Organization			
Process Implementation in Projects			
First Spot Check			
SCAMPI C Appraisal (Optional)			
Update Process Definitions			
Special Trainings (recommendations from Scampi C) (PM, Audit & Metrics)			
Second Spot Check			
SCAMPI B Appraisal			

CMMI Official CMMI training			
Documents Collection for final appraisal			
Readiness Review & ATM training			
Final set of Artifacts			
SCAMPI A Appraisal			
CMMI Sustenance Road Map			

In case if you are working for High Maturity Levels then add the following to your schedule,

a)   Process Capability Baselines Preparation

b)   Process Performance Model Development

c)   Business Objectives Fixing

d)   Business Objectives vs. Performance Evaluation

e)   Causal Analysis / Outcome Analysis Meetings

f)   High Maturity Reviews

g)   Quantitative Management Support activities

There are no timeline given here, because that's based on the organizations current maturity and gaps with respect to targeted maturity. However be clear if you don't have any previous experience with quality standards or don't have detailed Engineering or Services processes, then for Maturity Level 2, you may take 9 to 14 months and for Maturity Level 3, you may take 14 to 20 months, and for Maturity Level 4 or 5, you may take 24 to 38 months from the day you are appraised at Maturity Level 3. These all are indicative numbers and we recommend you not to take them as a hard and fast rule.

For your Process definition, plan a minimum of 3 to 6 months as duration. Plan your first spot check after 1.5 to 3 months after process training. Perform Scampi C, as you believe it will help. We will see in detail on SCAMPI C, B and A in the Appraisal Topic. Plan your second spot check after 2 to 4 months, after first spot check. Your final phase of Document update, SCAMPI planning, Readiness review and SCAMPI A will happen in last 3 months.

In High Maturity, Business Goal identification is the first activity. PCB development can be once in 6 month or in a year, it's based on lot of factors, we can see them in High Maturity section. PPM development shall start as early as possible. As the process is getting stable, initiate your Causal Analysis and Improvement Activities and ensure you have minimum 12 to 18 months to do better improvement.

Estimating Effort/Cost for CMMI Program:

Estimation of Effort in CMMI Program is typically performed with work break down structure method. Each task is allotted with effort based on the experience, its normal to check with your consultant on typically how much effort it will take. Also the estimate can be on Process QA group and Operational Members effort contribution, because most of the time your employees will ask what will be their level of effort involvement in this program.

Activity	Process Quality Assurance Group Effort	Others (SEPG/ Project teams/ Functions/FAR Group)
Lead Appraiser selection		
QMS Gap Study & Updation by Internal QA team		
QMS Gap Study By Lead Appraiser or by his/her Organization with respect to L3		

QMS Updation based on Gap Study Report (Including Alternate Practice Identification)		
Concentrated CMMI Implementation by SEPG Team		
CMMI Training for the Key Stakeholders		
First Spot Check		
SCAMPI C		
Process Definition Update		
Special Trainings (recommendations from SCAMPI C)		
Document Availability and Appraisal preparation		
Internal Appraisal		
Official CMMI training and SCAMPI Training		
PIID Development / Document Collection		
FAR Group identification		
SCAMPI B Appraisal		
Updating the Artifacts and Readiness Preparation		
SCAMPI A Appraisal		

The final effort can be presented in terms of Full time resource equivalent, though it has not much meaning for Operational teams, at least for management to calculate the cost it will be useful.

In addition don't forget to add the cost of your appraisal or consulting. Typically the cost goes from 20000$ to 45000$ for appraisal related activities. It's based on the services you avail and the scope of your appraisal and many other factors. The following appraisal related services, typically availed by organizations,

a)   SCAMPI C Appraisal

b)   SCAMPI B Appraisal

c)   SCAMPI A Appraisal

d)   CMMI Official Introduction Training

e)   ATM Training

f)   Readiness Review

g)   Intermediate Review

In Addition you may have consulting activities planned with identified Consulting partner (service providers). You have to include that cost also. Typical areas where you may need your consultant is,

a)   Training on Project Management, Reviews, Audits and Metrics

b)   Spot checks on Process Implementation

c)   Clarifications on Implementation

d)   Process Capability Baseline Development   Review

e)   Process Performance Models Development

f)   Sub Process Control – Clarifications

g)   Application of Causal Analysis

h)   Preparation for Appraisal

i)   Gap analysis on QMS

Having a consultant is not mandatory and it's optional, however when you have internal resources who can do this, you can go ahead with them. It's also common, that organizations bring external consultants, so that it helps in change management and reduces the internal frictions.

When organizations don't have process quality assurance teams, it's pretty common they outsource the work to external consultants. In that case, the competency required for performing the work differs and typically the cost for such work is lower than consulting.

For High Maturity Projects, you have to ensure that you may need to spend on tools. It's not mandatory to buy tools, there are freeware available and/or you can make your simple tools, which can support your needs. However as we know, freeware normally has its own limitations. Hence plan your budget accordingly. Few more details, we will on see on the High Maturity topic.

Stakeholder Management:

It's very important to identify and involve the stakeholders in this program. Sometimes, if you miss out anyone, this can hurt your team. So plan the stakeholders well, and establish clear communication with them. Normally we prepare the activities in Y axis and all the stakeholders in X axis. The participation level of them is entered in the relevant cells. It can be like a RACI matrix, where Responsible, Accountable, Consulted and Informed can be their Involvement in that activity.

Change Management:

To make any change at organizational level we need clear commitment from top management. If you get that, then you need a plan to introduce and grow that change in the organization. You need constant communication on the changes and bring more interest of people in that change. Ideally use all the milestone points in your program for better change management. Have a strong communication plan along with you, which reaches all levels of people in the organization. Appreciate the adoption of changes in every place, even you can create competition among internal units to ensure that change is accepted and implemented.

Your communication plan for CMMI program can have the following tasks with weekly/milestone based communication,

Sample Points of Communication	Mode of Communication
Communicate the Kick –off	Posters/Mail/Spot Event/Newsletters/Meeting/etc
Awareness Campaign (Select any topic)	
CMMI Training Completion - achievement	
CMMI Slogan Contest	
CMMI Status Report	
CMMI Awareness Topics	
CMMI Training Completion - Achievement of QMS Implementation Gap Analysis (SCAMPI C)	
QMS Completion and Release - Achievement	
Special Trainings Completion	
CMMI Awareness Topics	
CMMI Helpdesk Organizing	
QUIZ Program on CMMI	
CMMI Status - Audit Completion	

CMMI Status - Appraisal Completion	
SCAMPI B Schedule	
SCAMPI B Report	
SCAMPI A Schedule	
CMMI Maturity Level Achievement	
Sustenance Plan	

EXECUTING CMMI IMPLEMENTATION

Process Definition:

The base of this activity can be based on the Gap Analysis report, in case if you have existing defined processes. However if you don't have any existing processes, then it should start with discussion with your management team. Define the business goals of your organization, from there percolate it to process needs. The simpler and useful technique to have good process definition is, run it like development project, in the sense collect all the requirements with respect to your process needs, then make architecture for each process, its components and interface with other process, then develop the process along with relevant components and then validate with relevant Subject Matter Experts and with users.

Establish Requirements in a table,

Process Detail	Business Need	Type of Service	CMMI Practices	ISO/ISMS Needs	Policies/ Others
Req. Process	First time Sign off	ERP/NON ERP	Requirement Development Practices	Clause 7.1	Others
Design Process					

Coding process					

We can assign unique id and track the requirements.

Establish Design for the process,

    a) Description

    b) Interfaces (with other Process)

    c) Components (Templates, Guidelines, checklists, etc)

    d) Position in Overall process Architecture

    e) Entry Criteria

    f) Exit Criteria

Develop/Construct your Process,

The Process can be developed using ETVX methodology and with relevant components. ETVX – Entry, Task, Validation and Exit are the key details present in this method. In addition to that, we have other components which make that effective with this method.

The following can be the Process description details,

1 Objective

2 Scope

3 Entry Criteria

4 Acronyms and Abbreviations

5 Inputs

6 Process Description

 6.1 Activity 1

6.2 Activity 2

6.3 Activity 3

7 Recommendations

8 Permitted Tailoring

9 Measures

10 Validations

11 Quality Records

12 Exit Criteria

13 References (CMMI, Other Processes and Other Standards)

14 Process Profile Matrix

In addition to this you can have work flow for each process that will help the users in great way.

A process is not a standalone documents, as we know it has relevant components associated with it to make it more effective. The following can be considered as definitions for them,

Policy

It is a directive from senior management, on objectives and responsibilities for various aspects of the process.

In CMMI there is a practice GP 2.1 Establish Policy under Generic Goal 2, this is achieved by few organizations by making policy handbook or by writing the policy per process in the definition itself.

Process

It is a framework consisting of inputs, entry criteria, output, and exit criteria with list of activities/tasks to be performed to convert inputs to outputs. Process will contain certain templates and forms to be used while executing the activity/task. Process provides a mechanism for implementing certain policies and requirements of international standards/models facilitating Plan-Do-Check-Act approach to continual improvement

A process in your organization need not be the same as Process Area of CMMI. The Process needs and architecture is determined by various requirements you have identified. Some organizations just take the CMMI Specific practices in a Process Area and make them as practices; this may not really benefit them, as they don't understand the process architecture needs of them.

A Process of your organization may address multiple process Areas of CMMI and vice versa.

Standard

Standards specify uniform use of specific technologies, parameters or procedures when such use will benefit the organization. Ex: Coding Standards

Guidelines

Guidelines assist users in implementing policies/ procedures, which may warrant variations, or which are under trials and imposition of standards is not always achievable. Ex: Estimation Guideline

Procedures

Procedures assist in complying with applicable policies, standards and guidelines. They are detailed steps to be followed by users to accomplish a particular task. Procedures may contain certain templates to be followed while executing the task.

Templates

They are prescribed format for creating documents/deliverables expected by the processes. A well defined template helps us in achieving consistency in capturing information and reduces the redundancy.

Validation of process:

Validation of process happens through mostly reviews by relevant teams. The process is reviewed by Subject Matter Expert and then it's reviewed by SEPG team. A checklist based review by the author or his peer will help in reducing the defects. Similarly a traceability matrix from requirements through validation will help in reducing the defects.

Release of Process:

The following should be taken care on release of process,

a) Process and its components should have followed Naming Convention

b) Processes are reviewed and approved by SEPG

c) Relevant Training Records are updated

d) Processes are updated in QMS or in portal and ready for announcement

e) Process Transition plan is available

f) Process Request documents/requirements documents are updated

g) Master list of Processes are updated

h) Release Notes is prepared

i) Final Approval received from competent authority

j) Release communication is ready

Sometime people want to know, the different processes they should have, it's something which we can't answer easily, and it needs lot of context. I would recommend you to follow the method given above to come out with them.

Quality Management System Documents:

Every Quality management system contains quality manual as apex document, which provides detail on how the quality policy, objectives are achieved in the organization. The scope of processes, process architecture, and detail of every process is detailed in the manual. The Quality manual helps anyone to understand how the system is defined and helps to navigate the processes.

Quality Manual contains the following sections,

1.0 Introduction

 1.1 Purpose

 1.2 Scope

 1.3 References

 1.4 Definitions and Acronyms

2.0 Business Overview

 2.1 Business Group

 2.2 Vision/ Mission

 2.3 About Organization

 2.4 Nature of Business

 2.5 Organization Structure

 2.6 Business Objectives

3.0 Quality Management System

 3.1 Approach

 3.2 Documentation Structure

4.0 Quality Management Scope and Policy

 4.1 Scope of Quality Management System

 4.2 Quality Policy

5.0 Lifecycles

6.0 Tailoring of Processes

7.0 Quality Management Components

7.1 Management Review Committee/Steering Committee

7.2 SEPG

7.3 Policies

7.4 Procedures

7.5 Processes

7.6 Guidelines

7.7 Standards

Annexure: Process Architecture

Annexure: Process Details

Publishing Processes/QMS in Organization:

There are various methods by which the Processes/QMS is published within the organization. The simplest of them is having a common shared folder in a drive and give read only access to all members in the organization. Some uses wiki pages to publish interfaces and use databases or back end server to access the documents. Some organizations use share point portal for complete control on the QMS site. Some of them use intranet web portal as front end and use any available document management system as back end. What is important is, the QMS should have simple navigation and that requires good arrangement of documents. If you can create front end GUI interfaces, then it's good.

Some organizations use the Type of business (development, maintenance, testing) as the primary level document and subsequently lifecycles are given, from there processes are linked. In some organizations, even you can select all the relevant processes by the role. In some organizations you can select the processes by function. You have to select the relevant method, so that time spent on navigation can be reduced.

Roles and Responsibilities Documentation:

Well defined roles and responsibilities will help in reducing lot of ambiguities. The roles need not be designation offered in your organization. If you have the mapping to some extent, it's good, however don't allow people to get confused by designation. Roles have to be defined as you have identified in the processes and all the responsibilities given for the role in the processes shall be documented. Ensure that the roles required to perform some of the tasks as per the model is available with you. Example: Configuration activities shall be handled by a competent person in project, for that normally a configuration controller/manager role is identified. Check you have some role which is available to perform that activity. Unless you defined something at organizational level, it will never really get in to project level.

Maintenance of QMS:

The Quality Management System is maintained by the Process Quality Assurance group members in practical. However the responsibility lies with SEPG team. SEPG has to ensure all the processes are implemented and latest version is available for use by the users in the organization. A QMS revision can happen on need basis, as we get enough improvements/change requests coming in or based on following cases,

a) New Business Lines to be included

b) Change in Delivery model

c) Change in working methods

d) Changes in Tools/Technologies

e) Improvement Requests

f) Roles and Responsibility change

g) New Lifecycle

h) New Product line/service line

i) Audits/Compliance Standards triggered

j) Statutory or Regulatory compliances

k) Client Mandated changes

l) Others

The changes in QMS can be handled with planned releases in a year (like quarterly or half yearly), or we can handle them as they come. Hybrid approach is mostly used by organizations to handle QMS releases. Remember you can have all configuration practices applied for QMS, for better control.

One thing which we missed here is what is the QMS (Quality Management System) is all about, normally it's a system which is directed/guided in an organization to achieve quality in its products and services, and its comprises of roles, technology and processes. However over a period of time, people started recognizing QMS means, its set of processes in a shared place. In some companies they even refer QMS as Process QA group. However the intent of QMS has to be clearly understood, if not there will be problem in the basics itself.

Training in CMMI Program:

This is one of the Key components in this implementation program. It will take time and energy, but if we miss out this component, then all our implementation is only for the purpose of getting a rating, and also with lot of struggle. Training needs has to be determined clearly in every organization and time has to be allotted.

Training needs can be classified this way,

a) CMMI Model Training

b) Concepts Training (ex: Project Management, Configuration Management, Metrics ,Audit, Reviews, etc)

c) Process Training /QMS Training

d) Tools Training

e) High Maturity Training (For ML4 and ML5)

There are various modes of training available,

a) Instructor driven

b) E learning

c) Self Study

d) On the job

e) Coaching and so on

The better way to determine the training needs are based on, which role needs what training, using a simple table/matrix and get it checked with SEPG and SME's/Operations team

Role	Model Training	Concepts	Process/QMS	Tools	HM Training
Project Manager	CMMI v1.3 Dev CMMI v1.3 Svc	Project Management Estimation	Project Management	MS Project	Statistical Process Control
Developer	NA	Reviews	Coding	Review Tools	NA

We are not talking about technical trainings required for a role that depends on the project and its taken care by CMMI Process areas themselves, on how to determine and address them.

CMMI Institute offers many programs even for software development like Personal Software Process (PSP) and Team Software Process (TSP); however they are based on the need of the organizations to take.

Typically a well organized training program can go around 1 to 2 months, to ensure all relevant roles got trained. Typical duration of your training program can be 1 to 3 hrs, and in the need of long training hours, you can split them in to multiple days. Training programs can be organized with adequate exercises, quizzes and so on, to break the monotony. The fact is everyone has their normal work and taking large inputs in a day and applying it over a period of time, is difficult. Hence understanding this, you can split training programs in to multiple levels in different time periods.

Process Hand Holding Period:

Every team has a role to play in this, but the major role is played by the Operations team. They are the one, who actually implement the processes and provide feedback to organization. In a poor system, it will be always seen that Process QA group as the implementer of the process and/or it's for the Process QA group sake the Process related artifacts are produced. It's the operational team, who truly takes the responsibility, implement them, provide feedback and improve the processes to fit into the practical delivery needs of service/product. In some cases, we see operations teams are getting rewarded for following processes and achieving >80% compliance, we have nothing to say for that. It's expected that all the processes are complied by all the applicable projects, and even the case where they are not able to follow they have clear understanding of the situation and they are dealt in QMS in right way. Beyond everything, the success of CMMI Implementation program remains with the key implementation people, the operational team.

However it needs a good amount of facilitation from Process QA group, as most of the templates, guidelines are new to the Operation teams. The Process QA group can have dedicated period, like one to three months to help all the projects to implement the process and relevant components. There can be walkthrough sessions, clarifications session and review sessions to support the implementation. Similarly this is an important period for SEPG team to understand how the process deployment goes on. Wherever required they can release supportive guidelines, newsletters and communication to ensure successful Process implementation. The initial period is crucial for the program.

Always implement processes in multiple projects and don't go for pilot, once you have finalized your QMS, because getting feedback from different conditions and projects which has different characteristics is important. This helps in getting quick feedback and improving processes. However a caution can be made to projects, when really you are not sure about the process or you can go for piloting instead of a caution, but they should be based on adequate evaluation.

Key points in Execution of CMMI Implementation:

The following are some of the key points in execution, and since you already made a schedule they should be easier for you to implement,

a) Selection of Projects and/or Units: We have already decided at the beginning of this program that what kind of projects we want to cover in implementation, like application development, application maintenance, testing, migration, etc. Also this is the time to ensure that the scope of implementation remains same. Similarly check whether Package projects are part of your implementation. Once you have selected the type of projects and technology, then you can decide on the centers which are all following the same QMS, and how many those of you want to include in implementation. The reason is there could be very small centers and they don't produce/develop many services and including them in scope of implementation can have high impact in cost but not from benefit point of view. Remember here we are talking only about implementation of CMMI, not on appraisal. Implementation is for your business growth and for you delivery practices maturity, but appraisal is a stage in which you like to see whether you are doing alright when compared to external world and where your processes are good and where it can be improved. Sometimes we see organizations starting the implementation itself from appraisal point of view, which in larger picture is not the right thing and for your business it's not good. Similarly when selecting any center for implementation check on a) people b) Type of business c) Contribution to business d) technology available e) Connectivity f) Standardization need, etc. The reason is sometimes remote centers are there, and people are specialized in some area in that center, for them actually such implementation which you do at corporate level may not yield same level of benefit. Even they may feel it's too demanding, so you have to evaluate and then include them in Implementation. Basically whenever we talk on CMMI Implementation, most of the time we talk on process/QMS implementation, because apart from specific spot check/appraisals it's the processes which are defined in the organization is implemented by operational and support teams.

b) Broadcasting your program: Every stage in this program shall be broadcasted to the relevant members in the organization that will ensure the success of implementation. The more you keep the program within few members and few projects, in fact you are obstructing the implementation in full fledge. Involvement and belongingness shall be created by the level of communication you make. Involvement of senior management in such event is very important. Bring in methods like open forum discussion on monthly basis or stand up meeting on weekly/ bi weekly and involve all relevant stakeholders for 15 minutes or so. Discuss what you did in the last period and what the plan is for next period and what support you need from them. Not only this, but also discuss and attribute the success to operational teams. Neither the senior management nor the process quality assurance group needs any credit for the implementation, because for them its responsibility, however for operational team, it's something like change in culture and way of working and once they come in to process way of working, that's the best you can ask for. Be clear, we have to learn to appreciate others in this program than ourselves.

c) Implementation across Projects: The QMS should be implemented in all the applicable projects as discussed earlier. The best way is to create competition among different projects to implement processes quickly. A good support from QA facilitation team will help quick compliance. However it's also required the management people support process oriented approach. Often we see people searching to understand their process, only when client ask or when the quality compliant is received. The management people should be strong enough to ensure that every member is following process. This is very important when more than one member is working. Because you might be a hero to finish your work, but you don't know the other person is a hero to finish his/her works, at the same time, if you have thousands of employees, how can one identify all the heroes and allocate work. Instead believe in process, which will ensure expected level of consistency in results. Also it's important to ensure in appropriate phases the processes are implemented and relevant artifacts are produced. Sometime people allocate separate time for creating project artifacts for quality purpose; this is nothing but documentation work and will not yield real benefit. Some organization uses Quality Gates/Project gate mechanism based on milestones identified and relevant artifacts are checked and approved on that phase/period and then they are allowed to move to the next phase/milestone. This will ensure projects follow the applicable processes in the period. As discussed earlier the important benefit of implementing the processes across projects is to learn about the process on its ease of implementation, changes needed and elimination of complexity.

d) Compliance Checks: There are two levels of checks are performed in the process of implementation. (i) Audit activities to ensure the projects/work units (Work Unit terminology given here, so that CMMI SVC users can relate) are following all the relevant processes (ii) Appraisal/Spot Checks to ensure that CMMI Model practices are met. It is expected that already your QMS is completely covering all the CMMI practices, which means just by following your QMS; the CMMI practices expectations are met. However if your QMS is not well aligned then Audits may not be really that effective. Apart from that, we have to be clear that Audit as a technique is sample based and sometime the checklist (if any) doesn't address all the CMMI practices, which means by doing audit you may not be sure whether all practices are met in the organization. Also Audits may be designed in such a way that they only give non compliances, then again it's of less use to us. Appraisal is designed to evaluate the process in terms of strength and weakness based on a model/standard/some reference. Hence it's better to have both the approaches sometime to eliminate any gap in evaluation methodology. You may not do Audit and Appraisal together in same time for a project and you can plan it out with different period.

When any Spot checks are planned with external consultant, it's better to do an internal spot checks on your own. This will help in reducing the gaps and also your understanding and method of evaluation can be verified with external consultant. Otherwise your team learning such evaluation method is of reduced probability.

Normally you can concentrate on Specific practices of process areas in the first few checks in projects, apart from a QMS gap study on Generic practices. Which means, you are aware that you have generic practices are mapped in your Processes and in Quality management system, and also you are aware, when projects use your QMS the Generic practices will get satisfied, and knowing this you are concentrating on Specific practices. Some of the process areas can take some time to streamline, so it's better to concentrate on them (like measurement and analysis, decision analysis and resolution, etc)

e) Consulting Activities: If you have an external consultant, then it's better to create a log of questions to ask. You can keep it in central place, where different teams like SEPG, Process QA group, Operational teams, metrics team and others can update the log with their clarification needs. Prioritize them before you call your consultant and get it clarified with them. Many a times organization spends lot of time in template/guideline creation along with the consultant, this is not so effective way. You can ask your consultant to share some samples, and based on that you derive a model/and log questions where clarifications needed and just get it reviewed. CMMI is no longer an unknown phenomenon; there are sources available now a day to take templates to everything and the best sources is the web. A consultant need comes, when you need someone to provide multiple solutions to a given area, because of their rich experience in that area. In some cases, the consultant may be actually performing the dedicated SQA/outsourced SQA in that case, you can use his/her time for various activities as you plan. However when they are hired for providing guidance and solution, then we have to be clear with our need and problem. Also when it comes from various teams, it's more effective than one or two people thinking and deciding what to ask.

f) Typical Challenges & Risk Management: The Implementation challenges can be broadly classified in to (i) Model Interpretation (ii) Lifecycle Application (iii) Process Definition (iv) Implementation Challenge and (v) Miscellaneous. First thing which we need to do is classify our challenges in to the categories, and if you are able to do this level, then you are solution is half done. Model and Process definition challenges can be mostly addressed by your consultant or SME. The Implementation challenges shall be addressed by senior management, SEPG and steering committee. The Lifecycle application challenges can be addressed by the SEPG and Operational SME's. In addition to this, it's a good practice to have Risk log created for the CMMI program. The common issues given in the earlier topics can be taken as list of possible risk and evaluate it. Enter all the risks which your team foresees and do not shy away in entering any risk, as this a program for organization and it involves members from CEO to Developer. Track the risks periodically and discuss the top risks in the steering committee. Many a times we know a good risk management is equivalent of good program management.

g) Friction is good: The teams like SEPG, Process QA group, Metrics group and audit group might be having process people more. Sometimes the people are reporting to same functional head. This could trigger a case, where everyone is trying play down their role and taking care of their own people. Sometimes it might look all these are sub functions of one major process QA function and Operational teams will look completely as different group. If you don't see any friction between any of your internal groups mentioned above, it means you are having the best of the best or you are facing a real problem there. Each function when do their role effectively, there will be friction and issues, this a good sign and to be appreciated. Too much of friction good mean, they are just trying to safe guard themselves. Hence keep an eye on this Organizational dynamics.

Taking this opportunity lets discuss what SEPG is expected to perform typically,

- Establish and Maintain the Apex documents like Quality manual and policy up to date

- Establish and maintain Process Needs

- Establish and maintain process repository and process assets

- Deploy Processes and Process assets

- Appraise the Processes in the Organization

- Monitor and analyze Tailoring

- Improve the Processes

- Monitor Process alignment to meet business objectives

- Monitor and analyze Process Compliance

- Establish process action plans and execute them

Typically SEPG,

- To have its own plan for the year with clear planned schedule

- To have Clear roles and responsibilities

- Have configuration of documents

- Regular Meetings with action items tracking

- Analysis and decisions taken on meetings

- SEPG head shall be there to moderate and conduct sessions

Sample Work Breakdown Structure for SEPG,

Activity	Responsible	Month 1	Month 2	Month 'n'
Process Appraisal	Name 1	Yes		Yes
Internal Quality Audits (Refer Audit Calendar)				
Planned QMS Releases			Yes	
Lessons Learnt meetings		Yes	Yes	Yes
Process Improvement Reviews				
SEPG Measurement Analysis				
Risk Reviews				
Process Implementation Monitoring and Tracking				
Process Training - Need Analysis & Effectiveness Analysis				
Business Objectives tracking with Process				

Organizations' Tailoring and Process Asset - Analysis				
Reports to Senior Management				
Reports to Organization on deployment				
Incorporate Senior Management Review Feedback				
Process Compliance Review - For Monitoring Process and Process Assets usage in Projects				
Process Improvement Logs analysis				
Process Action plans tracking				

Process QA Group Activities:

Process QA group plays important role in ensuring that projects follow processes and healthy usage of process assets. Some of the activities of Process QA group given below,

• Handhold Projects on applying new processes and templates

• Project planning phase support

• Process QA reviews on internal/external deliverables to check on standards, procedure, templates & guidelines application (work product review of Process and Product quality assurance)

• Support on Metrics analysis

• Perform Audits (if audit team is part of the same group) on projects and follow relevant standards (you can follow ISO19011 based internal quality audit process)

- Track the non compliances coming out of Process QA reviews on deliverables and audits on process compliance, to closure

- Early warning analysis by Process QA group is possible based on Risks, project deviation from schedule , compliance level, etc can be performed with well defined reporting mechanism

- Final Deliverables check, sample configuration checks are other activities performed by Process QA group

- Support in Tailoring activities and maintenance of tailoring

Key points to note,

Process QA should not report to the Project manager, only an Indirect relationship should be there. Process QA should have a project level schedule to plan their deliverable review, and it could be part of the project schedule itself. Checklist based reviews and audits helps in establishing consistency; however it should not impact the investigative approach. Audits shall be based on Risk Impact approach, to ensure the points coming out of Audits are meaningful and well appreciated by operations team.

h) Spot Checks: These are the points in your CMMI Implementation, where you actually come to know where you have reached in this program. A well defined program can keep giving you the indicators that you are maturing in many areas, however if you haven't planned such tracking, then this is your evaluation point. Spot checks are performed by internal SME or by external consultant to evaluate the current level of meeting CMMI practices. This is ideally performed by selecting few projects from your implementation, which can demonstrate most of the phases in your development/services. The Projects are informed about the schedule and expectation well in advance to ensure their availability. The Spot check method includes, having a walk through with practitioner on relevant artifacts (outputs/documents) and asking them the clarifications.

Basically this method helps us to understand, for every relevant practice of CMMI, the Project has some or other artifact produced/evidenced and since the project team explains it, we believe that they have created/owns these artifacts as part of their project. This is a simple checking mechanism. Normally it takes 0.5 day to 1 day to have walkthrough with project. Similarly the support functions also included in it.

Sometimes the first few distinct type projects will be covered in detail and others will be checked only for few missing links.

Similarly it's not a bad idea to concentrate only on specific practices in first few spot checks and then slowly moving to Generic practices also.

Remember we are talking on practice level, it's only to say, that in practical life practices mentioned in CMMI are similar to tasks to achieve something. If we don't have some practice as mentioned in CMMI, we might have alternate practice. Similarly the goals are like activities in practical life, we can't miss out the activities, which just leads to failure. We address in this book at practice level, so that less clarifications are needed and more details are provided.

Spot Check Reports shall be at Practice Level. If the report doesn't give any remark on a practice, it means we assume that practice is well met in the samples taken.

Sample Report for Organizational Training Process Area,

Practice	Compliance	Gap
SP 1.1	Training needs are identified from SEPG (process related), projects (technical) and also from role based training needs; and feasible training programs	

		are rolled out	
SP 1.2		Project specific and org level trainings are planed and responsibilities are spelled out in Annual Training Plan	
SP 1.3		Annual Training Plan is established and maintained	
SP 1.4		Training capability is established through identification of trainers (internal and external), repository of training materials and training facilities Annual Training plan refers	
SP 2.1		Technical and Process trainings are conducted as per training calendar. Attendance records and training status reports are maintained	
SP 2.2		Training calendars, attendance records, feedback records are maintained	
SP 2.3		Training effectiveness is evaluated by analysis of training feedback	Action tracking based on analysis to be created.

Similarly if you can assign Compliance Level to each practice, you can get a score at Process Area level,

High – No Gap and complete compliance

Med- Few recommendations & no significant gap

Low- Significant gap in practice compliance

Now you can assign a rating of High = 1, Med = 0.5 and Low = 0

Now at Process Area level you can get compliance, like out 12 specific practices you have 4 high+ 6 Medium +2 Low => $4*1+6*0.5+2*0=>7$

This means, $7/12=> 59\%$ compliance

If you want you can go ahead and get compliance across all 22 (or) 24 process areas and take average out of them, which will give you a single figure like 62% compliance.

This is not a method suggested by CMMI Institute, however this helps us to quantify and get a rough value of where we stand in a moment. On subsequent Spot check, when we apply the same method, we get relative value of compliance. This helps us to see that we are moving well or not, again this is indicative only.

i)   Source of Process Improvements: There are various process improvement sources available in our organizations, they have to be identified and tracked continuously to improve our processes. The following are some of the sources,

   • Internal Audit Analysis

   • Tailoring Analysis

   • Metrics consolidated Analysis

   • Appraisal Reports

   • Client Feedbacks

   • Process QA facilitation reports

- Senior management inputs

- External Certification Audit reports

- Process Suggestion portals/Operation team requests

- Discussion forums organized in Organization

And other sources based on your organizational components.

j) Repositories Set Up: The processes used in the organization produces certain results and artifacts and these become important component for learning and for better preparation in further new projects. Repositories or Process Asset Repositories are helpful for the practitioners to get better prepared and to learn from experience of others. There are various repositories organizations maintain based on their need and effectiveness for delivery. Also it's a cost for organizations to set up and maintain repositories. A repository is normally created by collecting data from projects, analyzing them, filling the missing components, and standardizes the data in the required format, adding to database of the repository, having a front end which is easy to retrieve the information for projects and keep updating the repository over a period of time.

The following are the typical repositories maintained in organizations,

(i)   Measurement Repository

(ii)   Estimation Repository

(iii)   Defect Repository

(iv)   Service issues Repository

(v)   Risk Repository

(vi)   Lifecycle Repository

(vii)   Tailoring Repository

(viii)   Best Practices Repository

(ix)   Lessons Learnt Repository

(x)   Samples Repository

(xi)   Technical Know How – FAQ's

And other different repositories like reusable repository, domain specific repositories, etc

Every repository shall have an identified person allocated to maintain it. The data cleansing activity is performed, before adding the data to a repository. Adequate Communication in this regard will help better utilization. Some organizations use share point or web portal to publish their repositories, and counters are enabled to check how many clicks to the portal happened for the repository.

k)   CMMI Development Implementation - Typical Artifacts: The following can be considered as typical artifacts in normal life, organizations produce and which could meet the CMMI practices. Do not consider them as only documents and also by name and by content they could be merged and used also. Hence this is only for sample purpose only.

Process Area- Specific Goals & Specific Practices	Typical CMMI Artifact
Requirements Management	
SG 1 Manage Requirements	
SP 1.1 Understand Requirements	Requirements Document\ Collection of requirements & mails
SP1.2 Obtain Commitment to Requirements	Sign off on Requirement\agreement on requirements
SP 1.3 Manage Requirements Changes	Change log
SP 1.4 Maintain Bidirectional Traceability of Requirements	Traceability matrix
SP 1.5 Ensure Alignment between Project Work and Requirements	Updation of project plan

Requirements Development	
SG 1 Develop Customer Requirements	
SP 1.1 Elicit Needs	Requirements meeting MOM/prototype
SP 1.2 Transform Stakeholder needs into Customer Requirements	Business Requirements
SG 2 Develop Product Requirements	
SP 2.1 Establish Product and Product-Component Requirements	Software Requirements Specification document
SP 2.2 Allocate Product-Component Requirements	Software Requirements Specification document
SP 2.3 Identify Interface Requirements	Interface Requirements in SRS
SG 3 Analyze and Validate Requirements	
SP 3.1 Establish Operational Concepts and Scenarios	Use Case ,timeline scenarios, etc
SP 3.2 Establish a Definition of Required Functionality and Quality Attributes	activity diagram, use case
SP 3.3 Analyze Requirements	Requirements defect/review
SP 3.4 Analyze Requirements to Achieve Balance	Requirements allocation/module wise requirements, risks
SP 3.5 Validate Requirements	Analysis with client/prototype etc
Technical Solution	
SG 1 Select Product-Component Solutions	
SP 1.1 Develop Alternative Solutions and Selection Criteria	Alternative solutions/evaluation report/selection criteria
SP 1.2 Select Product-Component Solutions	Documented solution
SG 2 Develop the Design	
SP 2.1 Design the Product or Product Component	Product Architecture
SP 2.2 Establish a Technical Data Package	Technical data package
SP 2.3 Design Interfaces Using Criteria	Interface design/Criteria/Low Level design
SP 2.4 Perform Make or Buy Analysis	make/buy/reuse analysis

SG 3 Implement the Product Design	
SP 3.1 Implement the Design	Source code
SP 3.2 Develop Product Support Documentation	user manual/product manual
Product Integration	
SG 1 Prepare for Product Integration	
SP 1.1 Establish and Integration Strategy	Integration Strategy
SP 1.2 Establish the Product Integration Environment	Product integration strategy to have environment details
SP 1.3 Establish Product Integration Procedures and Criteria	Product integration plan
SG 2 Ensure Interface Compatibility	
SP 2.1 Review Interface Descriptions for Completeness	Integration review checklist
SP 2.2 Manage Interfaces	updated interfaces/MOM
SG 3 Assemble Product Components and Deliver the Product	
SP 3.1 Confirm Readiness of Product Components for Integration	Build readiness check
SP 3.2 Assemble Product Components	Build
SP 3.3 Evaluate Assembled Product Components	Release Readiness Checklist
SP 3.4 Package and Deliver the Product or Product Component	Release Note/Release
Verification	
SG 1 Prepare for Verification	
SP 1.1 Select Work Products for Verification	Reviews/Unit test plan
SP 1.2 Establish the Verification Environment	Templates/checklists/tools, etc
SP 1.3 Establish Verification Procedures and Criteria	Reviews/Unit test plan(procedure)
SG 2 Perform Peer Reviews	
SP 2.1 Prepare for Peer Reviews	peer review schedule/meeting planning, etc
SP 2.2 Conduct Peer Reviews	peer review report

SP 2.3 Analyze Peer Review Data	Defect closure
SG 3 Verify Selected Work Products	
SP 3.1 Perform Verification	Unit testing
SP 3.2 Analyze Verification Results and Identify Corrective Action	Defect Analysis & Defect prevention
Validation	
SG 1 Prepare for Validation	
SP 1.1 Select Products for Validation	System Test plan
SP 1.2 Establish the Validation Environment	Test Environment set up
SP 1.3 Establish Validation Procedures and Criteria	System Test plan
SG 2 Validate Product or Product Components	
SP 2.1 Perform Validation	Test Execution Results
SP 2.2 Analyze Validation Results	Defect Analysis & Defect prevention
Project Planning	
SG 1 Establish Estimates	
SP 1.1 Estimate the Scope of the Project	Top Level WBS, work Package description
SP 1.2 Establish Estimates of Work Product and Task Attributes	Size, estimating model
SP 1.3 Define Project Life Cycle	Life cycle documented (mostly in Project plan)
SP 1.4 Determine Estimates of Effort and Cost	Effort & cost of project (mostly in Project plan)
SG 2 Develop a Project Plan	
SP 2.1 Establish the Budget and Schedule	Budget and schedule (mostly Kick off/initiation deck etc)
SP 2.2 Identify Project Risks	Risk Identification checklist/Risk log
SP 2.3 Plan for Data Management	Data Management plan (mostly in project plan/charter)
SP 2.4 Plan for Project Resources	Project resources (mostly in project plan/charter)
SP 2.5 Plan for Needed Knowledge and Skills	Skill Matrix by roles
SP 2.6 Plan Stakeholder Involvement	Stakeholder Matrix
SP 2.7 Establish the Project	Project plan

Plan	
SG 3 Obtain Commitment to the Plan	
SP 3.1 Review Plans that Affect the Project	Revised plan/Review comments
SP 3.2 Reconcile Work and Resource Levels	Revised Plan
SP 3.3 Obtain Plan Commitment	Approval & Plan commitment from stakeholders
Project Monitoring and Control	
SG 1 Monitor Project Against Plan	
SP 1.1 Monitor Project Planning Parameters	Effort, schedule, other measures (Metrics report)
SP 1.2 Monitor Commitments	Commitment monitoring (Meeting MOM/issues, etc)
SP 1.3 Monitor Project Risks	Risk Log/weekly/biweekly/monthly reports
SP 1.4 Monitor Data Management	Data Confidentiality/availability and integrity monitoring (Meeting MOM)
SP 1.5 Monitor Stakeholder Involvement	Stakeholder participation (Meeting MOM)
SP 1.6 Conduct Progress Reviews	Monthly reviews/biweekly reviews
SP 1.7 Conduct Milestone Reviews	Milestone meeting (Sometimes Monthly/biweekly reviews)
SG 2 Manage Corrective Action to Closure	
SP 2.1 Analyze Issues	Issue Log
SP 2.2 Take Corrective Action	Action items (mostly in MOM or in a log/tool)
SP 2.3 Manage Corrective Action	Action Closure status and details (mostly in MOM or in a log/tool)
Risk Management	
SG 1 Prepare for Risk Management	
SP 1.1 Determine Risk Sources and Categories	Risk Source and category (can be part of Risk log/sheet and applied to each risk)
SP 1.2 Define Risk Parameters	Risk Parameters typically impact * probability =>Risk Exposure
SP 1.3 Establish a Risk Management Strategy	Strategy document/guidance in Risk log itself (threshold/mitigation/contingency/acc

	eptance/avoidance/roles)
SG 2 Identify and Analyze Risks	
SP 2.1 Identify Risks	List of Identified risks (risk log)
SP 2.2 Evaluate Risks	Risk Exposure and priority
SG 3 Mitigate Risks	
SP 3.1 Develop Risk Mitigation Plans	Mitigation actions (to reduce risk exposure- mostly in risk log)
SP 3.2 Implement Risk Mitigation Plans	Action closure and Risk rating modifications
Configuration Management	
SG 1 Establish Baselines	
SP 1.1 Identify Configuration Items	Configurable items list (mostly in Configuration plan)
SP 1.2 Establish a Configuration Management System	Configuration repository, approval mechanism (mostly in configuration Plan)
SP 1.3 Create or Release Baselines	Baselines list/criteria (mostly in configuration plan)
SG 2 Track and Control Changes	
SP 2.1 Track Change Requests	Change requests logged
SP 2.2 Control Configuration Items	Change requests status update
SG 3 Establish Integrity	
SP 3.1 Establish Configuration Management Records	Status Accounting /configuration history reports
SP 3.2 Perform Configuration Audits	Configuration audit(functional/physical)
Measurement and Analysis	
SG 1 Align Measurement and Analysis Activities	
SP 1.1 Establish Measurement Objectives	Define measurement objectives (org level can be mapped to project level)
SP 1.2 Specify Measures	Effort/defect/schedule/utilization, etc
SP 1.3 Specify Data Collection and Storage Proc	data source, collection, frequency(metric guideline/report itself)
SP 1.4 Specify Analysis Procedures	procedure to analyze (graphs/chart/points to consider)
SG 2 Provide Measurement Results	
SP 2.1 Obtain Measurement Data	Metrics Report
SP 2.2 Analyze Measurement	Metrics Report

Data	
SP 2.3 Store Data and Results	Metrics Report
SP 2.4 Communicate Results	Meeting minutes/monthly/bimonthly reports
Process and Product Quality Assurance	
SG 1 Objectively Evaluate Processes and Work Products	
SP 1.1 Objectively Evaluate Processes	Audit report (Process Audit)
SP 1.2 Objectively Evaluate Work Products and Services	Work product Review Report (SQA review on deliverables)
SG 2 Provide Objective Insight	
SP 2.1 Communicate and Ensure Resolution of NC Issues	Non compliance closure Report
SP 2.2 Establish Records	Non compliance closure Report
Integrated Project Management	
SG 1 Use the Project's Defined Process	Tailoring
SP 1.1 Establish the Project's Defined Process	tailoring checklist/document (of organization process with project context)
SP 1.2 Use Organizational Process Assets for Planning Project Activities	estimation/measurements/risks, etc used for planning (mostly in project plan)
SP 1.3 Establish Project's work Environment	Documented Project environment (mostly in project plan)
SP 1.4 Integrate Plans	integrated project plan
SP 1.5 Manage the Project Using the Integrated Plans	Revised integrated project plan/updates based on it
SP 1.6 Establish Teams	Team roles and guidance (Mostly in project plan)
SP 1.7 Contribute to the Organizational Process Assets	Lessons learnt/best practices/improvements, etc
SG 2 Coordinate and Collaborate with Relevant Stakeholders	
SP 2.1 Manage Stakeholder Involvement	Team Meetings/issue log/Project meetings
SP 2.2 Manage Dependencies	Issue ,dependency log & closure of actions
SP 2.3 Resolve Coordination	Issue ,dependency log & closure of

Issues	actions
Organizational Training	
SG 1 Establish an Organizational Training Capability	
SP 1.1 Establish the Strategic Training Needs	Linked training needs with business objectives (mostly annual Training plan /strategy document)
SP 1.2 Determine Which Training Needs Are the Responsibility of the Organization	Project level & Org level training - listed (in plan)
SP 1.3 Establish an Organizational Training Tactical Plan	Training Calendar
SP 1.4 Establish Training Capability	Training environment, trainer details documented at org. level
SG 2 Provide Necessary Training	
SP 2.1 Deliver Training	Training delivery record (Invite/material/feedback/attendance)
SP 2.2 Establish Training Records	Training delivery record (Invite/material/feedback)
SP 2.3 Assess Training Effectiveness	Training feedback evaluation/360 feedback/performance check, etc
Organizational Process Focus	
SG 1 Determine Process-Improvement Opportunities	
SP 1.1 Establish Organizational Process Needs	Process Needs & details (mostly in Quality Manual)
SP 1.2 Appraise the Organization's Processes	Audit/appraise/review organization process
SP 1.3 Identify the Organization's Process Improvements	Improvement log (based on appraisals and from projects)
SG 2 Plan and Implement Process Actions	
SP 2.1 Establish Process Action Plans	Improvement Log (with CR/improvement and action plan)
SP 2.2 Implement Process Action Plans	Improvement Log status(with CR/improvement and action plan)
SG 3 Deploy Organizational Process Assets and Incorporate experiences	
SP 2.1 Deploy Organizational	Deployment plan with status

Process Assets	
SP 2.2 Deploy standard processes	Deployment plan with status
SP 2.3 Monitor the Implementation	Deployment plan with status
SP 2.4 Incorporate Experiences into the Organizational Process Assets	Updated Repositories (Estimation/risk/defects/samples, etc)
Organizational Process Definition	
SG 1 Establish Organizational Process Assets	Define Processes
SP 1.1 Establish Standard Processes	Documented process Definitions
SP 1.2 Establish Life-Cycle Model Descriptions	Lifecycle description (waterfall/incremental/iterative, etc)
SP 1.3 Establish Tailoring Criteria and Guidelines	Tailoring Guideline (mostly by process) and Criteria (small/large, etc)
SP 1.4 Establish the Organization's Measurement Repository	Metrics repository
SP 1.5 Establish the Organization's Process Asset Library	Repositories (Estimation/risk/defects/samples, etc)
SP 1.6 Establish work Environment Standards	Work Environment details (mostly in Quality manual)
SP 1.7 Establish rules and guidelines for teams	Teaming norms (mostly in Quality manual)
Decision Analysis and Resolution	
SG 1 Evaluate Alternatives	
SP 1.1 Establish Guidelines for Decision Analysis	Guideline (when to use, criteria, responsible, etc)
SP 1.2 Establish Evaluation Criteria	Criteria to evaluate decision(it will vary based on the context)
SP 1.3 Identify Alternative Solutions	Document alternate solution (separate DAR sheet used in many org.)
SP 1.4 Select Evaluation Methods	Evaluation techniques (Pugh matrix, cost benefit, weighted average, etc) (DAR sheet to have the method)
SP 1.5 Evaluate Alternatives	Valuation of each alternative solution (DAR sheet)

SP 1.6 Select Solutions	Final Solution (DAR sheet)

l) CMMI Services Implementation –Typical Artifacts: The following can be considered as typical artifacts in normal life, organizations produce and which could meet the CMMI practices. Do not consider them as only documents and also by name and by content they could be merged and used also. Hence this is only for sample purpose only.

Process Area- Specific Goals & Specific Practices	Typical CMMI Artifact
Configuration Management	
SG 1 Establish Baselines	
SP 1.1 Identify Configuration Items	Configurable items list (mostly in Configuration plan)
SP 1.2 Establish a Configuration Management System	Configuration repository, approval mechanism (mostly in configuration Plan)
SP 1.3 Create or Release Baselines	Baselines list/criteria (mostly in configuration plan)
SG 2 Track and Control Changes	
SP 2.1 Track Change Requests	Change requests logged
SP 2.2 Control Configuration Items	Change requests status update
SG 3 Establish Integrity	
SP 3.1 Establish Configuration Management Records	Status Accounting /configuration history reports
SP 3.2 Perform Configuration Audits	Configuration audit(functional/physical)
Measurement and Analysis	
SG 1 Align Measurement and Analysis Activities	
SP 1.1 Establish Measurement Objectives	Define measurement objectives (org level can be mapped to project level)
SP 1.2 Specify Measures	Effort/defect/schedule/utilization, etc
SP 1.3 Specify Data Collection and Storage Procedures	data source, collection, frequency(metric guideline/report itself)
SP 1.4 Specify Analysis	procedure to analyze

Procedures	(graphs/chart/points to consider)
SG 2 Provide Measurement Results	
SP 2.1 Obtain Measurement Data	Metrics Report
SP 2.2 Analyze Measurement Data	Metrics Report with Analysis
SP 2.3 Store Data and Results	Metrics Report in Database & Communication
SP 2.4 Communicate Results	Meeting minutes/monthly/bimonthly reports
Process and Product Quality Assurance	
SG 1 Objectively Evaluate Processes and Work Products	
SP 1.1 Objectively Evaluate Processes	Audit report (Process Audit) with Noncompliance & corrective actions Audit checklist
SP 1.2 Objectively Evaluate Work Products	Process QA Review Report
SG 2 Provide Objective Insight	
SP 2.1 Communicate and Resolve Noncompliance Issues	Non compliance closure Report Mail of report being shared with stakeholders
SP 2.2 Establish Records	Audit plan Non compliance closure Report Status of corrective actions
Requirements Management	
SG 1 Manage Requirements	
SP 1.1 Understand Requirements	Requirements Document\ Collection of requirements & mails
SP 1.2 Obtain Commitment to Requirements	Sign off on Requirement\agreement on requirements
SP 1.3 Manage Requirements Changes	Change log
SP 1.4 Maintain Bidirectional Traceability of Requirements	Service Requirements traceability matrix Requirements tracking system
SP 1.5 Ensure Alignment between Work Products and Requirements	Updation of project plan
Supplier Agreement Management	

SG 1 Establish Supplier Agreements	
SP 1.1 Determine Acquisition Type	Type of Suppliers and Acquisition types
SP 1.2 Select Suppliers	Supplier list and Vendor Evaluation sheet
SP 1.3 Establish Supplier Agreements	Purchase Order, Contract, SOW
SG 2 Satisfy Supplier Agreements	
SP 2.1 Execute the Supplier Agreement	Receive Product, Track Supply - Tracking status
SP 2.2 Accept the Acquired Product	Acceptance report, inception report
SP 2.3 Ensure Transition of Products	Transition plans, handover report Training reports
Service Delivery	
SG 1 Establish Service Agreements	
SP 1.1 Analyze Existing Agreements and Service Data	Analysis of past SLA's and SOW & Analysis of reports
SP 1.2 Establish the Service Agreement	Service agreement/ Contract etc
SG 2 Prepare for Service Delivery	
SP 2.1 Establish the Service Delivery Approach	Project/Service management plan with the agreed Service delivery approach (Incident/problem, etc)
SP 2.2 Prepare for Service System Operations	Validation of Knowledge Transfer/ Validation of Service System tool (training etc)/ operational readiness assessment
SP 2.3 Establish a Request Management System	Incident Management tool/ Log
SG 3 Deliver Services	
SP 3.1 Receive and Process Service Requests	Incident Management record in the tool/ Log
SP 3.2 Operate the Service System	Service logs from the tool/ Performance Status reports
SP 3.3 Maintain the Service System	Corrective or preventive maintenance change requests/ Change Requests on the service system
Work Planning	

SG 1 Establish Estimates	
SP 1.1 Establish the Service Strategy	Service Strategy Document
SP 1.2 Estimate the Scope of the Work	Top Level WBS, work Package description
SP 1.3 Establish Estimates of Work Product and Task Attributes	Size, estimating model
SP 1.4 Define Lifecycle Phases	Life cycle documented (mostly in Project /Service management plan)
SP 1.5 Estimate Effort and Cost	Effort & cost of project (mostly in Project plan)
SG 2 Develop a Work Plan	
SP 2.1 Establish the Budget and Schedule	Budget and schedule (mostly Kick off/initiation deck etc)
SP 2.2 Identify Risks	Risk Identification checklist/Risk log
SP 2.3 Plan Data Management	Data Management plan (mostly in project plan/charter)
SP 2.4 Plan the Resources	Project resources (mostly in project plan/charter)
SP 2.5 Plan Needed Knowledge and Skills	Skill Matrix by roles
SP 2.6 Plan Stakeholder Involvement	Stakeholder Matrix
SP 2.7 Establish the Work Plan	Project plan/Service Management Plan
SG 3 Obtain Commitment to the Plan	
SP 3.1 Review Plans That Affect the Work	Revised plan/Review comments
SP 3.2 Reconcile Work and Resource Levels	Revised Plan
SP 3.3 Obtain Plan Commitment	Approval & Plan commitment from stakeholders
Work Monitoring and Control	
SG 1 Monitor the Work Against the Plan	
SP 1.1 Monitor Work Planning Parameters	Effort, schedule, other measures (Metrics report)
SP 1.2 Monitor Commitments	Commitment monitoring (Meeting MOM/issues, etc)
SP 1.3 Monitor Risks	Risk Log/weekly/biweekly/monthly reports
SP 1.4 Monitor Data	Data Confidentiality/availability and

Management	integrity monitoring (Meeting MOM)
SP 1.5 Monitor Stakeholder Involvement	Stakeholder participation (Meeting MOM)
SP 1.6 Conduct Progress Reviews	Monthly reviews/biweekly reviews
SP 1.7 Conduct Milestone Reviews	Milestone meeting (Sometimes Monthly/biweekly reviews)
SG 2 Manage Corrective Action to Closure	
SP 2.1 Analyze Issues	Issue Log
SP 2.2 Take Corrective Action	Action items (mostly in MOM or in a log/tool)
SP 2.3 Manage Corrective Actions	Action Closure status and details (mostly in MOM or in a log/tool)
Capacity and Availability Management	
SG 1 Prepare for Capacity and Availability Management	
SP 1.1 Establish a Capacity and Availability Management Strategy	Service management plan with details on Human/Infra/technological capacity and availability for agreed service
SP 1.2 Select Measures and Analytic Techniques	Capacity and availability measures and analysis technique
SP 1.3 Establish Service System Representations	process simulation (system simulation), Simulation of inflow and capacity and availability with excel
SG 2 Monitor and Analyze Capacity and Availability	
SP 2.1 Monitor and Analyze Capacity	Trend charts on service resource usage data
SP 2.2 Monitor and Analyze Availability	Trends on availability, analysis and action
SP 2.3 Report Capacity and Availability Management Data	Service system performance reports Service availability reports
Decision Analysis and Resolution	
SG 1 Evaluate Alternatives	
SP 1.1 Establish Guidelines for Decision Analysis	Guideline (when to use, criteria, responsible, etc)
SP 1.2 Establish Evaluation Criteria	Criteria to evaluate decision(it will vary based on the context)
SP 1.3 Identify Alternative	Document alternate solution (separate

Solutions	DAR sheet used in many org.)
SP 1.4 Select Evaluation Methods	Evaluation techniques (Pugh matrix, cost benefit, weighted average, etc) (DAR sheet to have the method)
SP 1.5 Evaluate Alternative Solutions	Valuation of each alternative solution (DAR sheet)
SP 1.6 Select Solutions	Final Solution (DAR sheet)
Incident Resolution and Prevention	
SG 1 Prepare for Incident Resolution and Prevention	
SP 1.1 Establish an Approach to Incident Resolution and Prevention	SQP with details on Service Incident handling approach
SP 1.2 Establish an Incident Management System	Service Incident logging Tool/ Log
SG 2 Identify, Control, and Address Individual Incidents	
SP 2.1 Identify and Record Incidents	Service Incident ticket record
SP 2.2 Analyze Individual Incident Data	Major incident, repeat incident analysis
SP 2.3 Resolve Incidents	Updated resolution in the tool/ log
SP 2.4 Monitor the Status of Incidents to Closure	Closure Service incident log/ Status update/ Escalation data (mail/tool ref etc)
SP 2.5 Communicate the Status of Incidents	Status reports/ Communication mail
SG 3 Analyze and Address Causes and Impacts of Selected Incidents	
SP 3.1 Analyze Selected Incidents	Report of underlying causes of incidents/ Documented causal analysis activities
SP 3.2 Establish Solutions to Respond to Future Incidents	Knowledge data base
SP 3.3 Establish and Apply Solutions to Reduce Incident Occurrence	Change in Service Delivery system like a tool/ procedure / policies etc.
Service System Transition	
SG 1 Prepare for Service System Transition	
SP 1.1 Analyze Service	Compatibility analysis of current and

System Transition Needs	post-transition service systems Baseline service system components Mitigations for of identified transition Issues and risks
SP 1.2 Develop Service System Transition Plans	Transition plans for service system transition (tools, process, competency)
SP 1.3 Prepare Stakeholders for Changes	Strategy of training and transition Transition communication and notification artifacts (e.g., emails, system announcements, bulletin boards)
SG 2 Deploy the Service System	
SP 2.1 Deploy Service System Components	Installation records Installation instructions Operational scenarios and procedures
SP 2.2 Assess and Control the Impacts of the Transition	Post deployment review Back out / rollback results, if needed Service impacts due to deployment issues
Service System Development	
SG 1 Develop and Analyze Stakeholder Requirements	
SP 1.1 Develop Stakeholder Requirements	Customer requirements End-user requirements
SP 1.2 Develop Service System Requirements	Service system Requirements & software requirement specification
SP 1.3 Analyze and Validate Requirements	Prototype, Validation of requirements
SG 2 Develop Service Systems	
SP 2.1 Select Service System Solutions	Architecture of solution, Service system design
SP 2.2 Develop the Design	Code and develop service software, develop components of service system
SP 2.3 Ensure Interface Compatibility	Interface identification within components and external components of service system
SP 2.4 Implement the Service System Design	Implemented service system components Training materials User, operator, and maintenance

	manual
SP 2.5 Integrate Service System Components	Service system integration plan, build the service system
SG 3 Verify and Validate Service Systems	
SP 3.1 Prepare for Verification and Validation	Verification tools, environment, test strategy, simulation plan
SP 3.2 Perform Peer Reviews	peer review checklist, peer review report
SP 3.3 Verify Selected Service System Components	Review and unit test
SP 3.4 Validate the Service System	Validation reports and results, Test Results
Integrated Work Management	
SG 1 Use the Defined Process for the Work	
SP 1.1 Establish the Defined Process	tailoring checklist/document (of organization process with project context)
SP 1.2 Use Organizational Process Assets for Planning Work Activities	estimation/measurements/risks, etc used for planning (mostly in project plan)
SP 1.3 Establish the Work Environment	Documented Project environment (mostly in project plan)
SP 1.4 Integrate Plans	integrated project plan
SP 1.5 Manage the Work Using Integrated Plans	Revised integrated project plan/updates based on it
SP 1.6 Establish Teams	Team roles and guidance (Mostly in project plan)
SP 1.7 Contribute to Organizational Process Assets	Lessons learnt/best practices/improvements, etc
SG 2 Coordinate and Collaborate with Relevant Stakeholders	
SP 2.1 Manage Stakeholder Involvement	Team Meetings/issue log/Project meetings
SP 2.2 Manage Dependencies	Issue ,dependency log & closure of actions
SP 2.3 Resolve Coordination Issues	Issue ,dependency log & closure of actions
Strategic Service Management	

SSG 1 Establish Strategic Needs and Plans for Standard Services	
SP 1.1 Gather and Analyze Data	Analyzed data on the organization's capabilities (past performance report) Analyzed data on strategic needs, Analysis report
SP 1.2 Establish Plans for Standard Services	Strategic plan on standard service, catalogue, needs
SG 2 Establish Standard Services	
SP 2.1 Establish Properties of Standard Services and Service Levels	Critical attributes of standard services Organization's set of standard service levels Common and variable parts of standard services
SP 2.2 Establish Descriptions of Standard Services	Service Catalog with specific instructions
Service Continuity	
SG 1 Identify Essential Service Dependencies	
SP 1.1 Identify and Prioritize Essential Functions	Risk Assessment, Business continuity assessment report
SP 1.2 Identify and Prioritize Essential Resources	prioritization based on Assessment (Business continuity assessment report)
SG 2 Prepare for Service Continuity	
SP 2.1 Establish Service Continuity Plans	Business Continuity plan
SP 2.2 Establish Service Continuity Training	Service continuity training material Training records
SP 2.3 Provide and Evaluate Service Continuity Training	Training Records on business continuity
SG 3 Verify and Validate the Service Continuity Plan	
SP 3.1 Prepare for the Verification and Validation of the Service Continuity Plan	Plan for Business continuity check
SP 3.2 Verify and Validate the Service Continuity Plan	Review report

SP 3.3 Analyze Results of Verification and Validation of the Service Continuity Plan	Results of Simulation Test report & improvement recommendations
Risk Management	
SG 1 Prepare for Risk Management	
SP 1.1 Determine Risk Sources and Categories	Risk Source and category (can be part of Risk log/sheet and applied to each risk)
SP 1.2 Define Risk Parameters	Risk Parameters typically impact * probability =>Risk Exposure
SP 1.3 Establish a Risk Management Strategy	Strategy document/guidance in Risk log itself (threshold/mitigation/contingency/acc eptance/avoidance/roles)
SG 2 Identify and Analyze Risks	
SP 2.1 Identify Risks	List of Identified risks (risk log)
SP 2.2 Evaluate, Categorize, and Prioritize Risks	Risk Exposure and priority
SG 3 Mitigate Risks	
SP 3.1 Develop Risk Mitigation Plans	Mitigation actions (to reduce risk exposure- mostly in risk log)
SP 3.2 Implement Risk Mitigation Plans	Action closure and Risk rating modifications
Organizational Training	
SG 1 Establish an Organizational Training Capability	
SP 1.1 Establish Strategic Training Needs	Linked training needs with business objectives (mostly annual Training plan /strategy document)
SP 1.2 Determine Which Training Needs Are the Responsibility of the Organization	Project level & Org level training - listed (in plan)
SP 1.3 Establish an Organizational Training Tactical Plan	Training Calendar
SP 1.4 Establish a Training Capability	Training environment, trainer details documented at org. level
SG 2 Provide Training	
SP 2.1 Deliver Training	Training delivery record

	(Invite/material/feedback/attendance)
SP 2.2 Establish Training Records	Training delivery record (Invite/material/feedback)
SP 2.3 Assess Training Effectiveness	Training feedback evaluation/360 feedback/performance check, etc
Organizational Process Focus	
SG 1 Determine Process Improvement Opportunities	
SP 1.1 Establish Organizational Process Needs	Process Needs & details (mostly in Quality Manual)
SP 1.2 Appraise the Organization's Processes	Audit/appraise/review organization process
SP 1.3 Identify the Organization's Process Improvements	Improvement log (based on appraisals and from projects)
SG 2 Plan and Implement Process Actions	
SP 2.1 Establish Process Action Plans	Improvement Log (with CR/improvement and action plan)
SP 2.2 Implement Process Action Plans	Improvement Log status(with CR/improvement and action plan)
SG 3 Deploy Organizational Process Assets and Incorporate Experiences	
SP 3.1 Deploy Organizational Process Assets	Deployment plan with status
SP 3.2 Deploy Standard Processes	Deployment plan with status
SP 3.3 Monitor the Implementation	Deployment plan with status
SP 3.4 Incorporate Experiences into Organizational Process Assets	Updated Repositories (Estimation/risk/defects/samples, etc)
Organizational Process Definition	
SG 1 Establish Organizational Process Assets	Define Processes
SP 1.1 Establish Standard Processes	Documented process Definitions
SP 1.2 Establish Life-Cycle	Lifecycle description

Model Descriptions	(waterfall/incremental/iterative, etc)
SP 1.3 Establish Tailoring Criteria and Guidelines	Tailoring Guideline (mostly by process) and Criteria (small/large, etc)
SP 1.4 Establish the Organization's Measurement Repository	Metrics repository
SP 1.5 Establish the Organization's Process Asset Library	Repositories (Estimation/risk/defects/samples, etc)
SP 1.6 Establish Work Environment Standards	Work Environment details (mostly in Quality manual)
SP 1.7 Establish Rules and Guidelines for Teams	Teaming norms (mostly in Quality manual)

m) Generic Goals/Practices

Generic Goals & Practices	Typical Artifacts
GG2: Institutionalize a Managed process	
GP2.1 Establish an Organizational Policy	Policy guide book/ policy within a process
GP2.2 Plan the process	Part of work break down structure
GP2.3 Provide resources	Resource allocation in Project plan/Service management plan
GP2.4 Assign Responsibility	Roles and Responsibility in Project plan/Service management plan
GP2.5 Train People	Skill matrix and training plan
GP2.6 Control work products	Configuration plan with Configurable items
GP2.7 Identify and Involve Relevant Stakeholders	Stakeholder management plan/matrix with tasks in Project/Service management plan

GP2.8 Monitor and Control the process	Metrics report/capacity report/meeting minutes
GP2.9 Objectively Evaluate Adherence	Audit reports for all processes
GP2.10 Review Status with Higher Level Management	Status reports/MOM ,etc
GG 3 Institutionalize a Defined Process	
GP3.1 Establish a defined Process	Process Description and Tailoring details for process in a project
GP3.2 Collect Process related experiences	Process lessons learnt, data from process, etc

The Generic practices should be applied for each of process area with that context. Here whatever we have given is a sample, if you try to understand that this will fit everywhere it's a Risk. Hence·be cautious this is only for sample purpose.

n) Monitoring and Control of program: The Monitoring of the program is an important activity and should be continuous. As we discussed earlier, we have steering committee and we have SEPG running, however it's important for the CMMI program manager to keep track of the happenings as per the schedule and generating the relevant measures in alignment with program management parameters.

It starts from reporting the schedule deviation and effort deviation; some organizations use earned value analysis method to show the overall deviation on schedule and effort. Some people may claim that effort can be estimated in a program like CMMI, however in normal life there are companies who have estimated effort, tracked and controlled it (not FTE). Estimation can always be revised, but what it makes you is taking decision in informed way. Considering the spot check compliance rating method we described earlier, you can go ahead and have targets for your CMMI compliance level by each spot check/appraisal, and see whether you are in that range.

Ex: Spot check 1, you wanted to achieve 55% compliance and spot check 2, you wanted to achieve 65% compliance etc. similarly before the appraisal, and you may want to reach more than 95% compliance with the model.

Other monitoring is on the deliverables by timeline. If you have targeted QMS release on a particular period to support the implementation, any delay will have impact on the successor task in your schedule.

Communication of the Metrics report and compliance chart publishing in various places in the organization will give confidence and the information to employees and encourages them to progress further.

o) Other Points to take care in Implementation:

- Monitor the scope of implementation throughout and not to deviate

- The barriers has to be logged in issue log, but keep progressing in other areas ,while clearing them

- Check the coverage level in implementation

- Check the compliance level in implementation

- Don't go for any short cut, that's not what is intended by your organizations. Work around is different from short cuts.

- Be ready to face the challenges and don't shy away from them

- Be proactive and drive the implementation and don't allow the program to drive you.

- The time limit set should be always challenging than comfort, however too aggressive timeline can be devastating also. Always go for 20% more than your comfort zone.

- Strong Management support is very important, because not every question can be answered with data or history, new things has to be experimented, and whenever you face challenges that people are not ready for change, and then management support is vital.

- You may progress slower than what you aimed for, but if the progress is convincing and meaningful results are coming out, then don't worry about them.

- Manage the Ego between people, this is important for success. This is anyway part of change management, however ego and personal goal clashes sometime hinders the progress of the program. You have to ready to convince and include them sometime, or escalate as needed or change few things in organization to ensure that dynamics settles well to produce a supportive environment.

- Never allocate a person to run a CMMI program, because they are free or you want them to work hard. You need a person, who is strategic and who can ensure that every arm is working towards the goal. Sometimes we see people, who are not very successful in delivery is suddenly allocated to this program to manage. The reality is this the important program in your organization and it's going to change your culture, then why to allocate a poorly performing person there. However if you believe this only for achieving some rating and you are not going to change anything, it means you are already decided the failure, so feel free to allocate anyone.

- Never call it as "Certification". This is clarified many times by SEI and now by CMMI Institute that there is nothing like Certification at organization level. But still we see organizations calling it as certification. This is more than just wording, it reflects the mentality and approach they have over the program. It's only a "Rating" based on Appraisal on Maturity or capability level on that instance of appraisal. Every time correct your employees when they use the word certification, this is important for them to understand and live up to the expectation of the program.

Execution of all the tasks mentioned in your plan as per the suggestions given here will definitely lead you to a better position and to get ready for your appraisal.

APPRAISING CMMI IMPLEMENTATION

This is an important phase to evaluate your processes and understand the strength and weaknesses and find the improvement opportunities to increase the efficiency and effectiveness of your processes. Also it gives a way to bench mark and see your process maturity level across industry through appraisal rating system.

Appraisal phase has lot of different activities and terminologies to understand for better clarity. To Appraise the CMMI Model, there is a document called "ARC – Appraisal Requirements for CMMI" is available, which basically explains the different criteria and characteristics the appraisal method should posses. We are not much bothered about it, as CMMI Institute has an Appraisal Method called SCAMPI which is already in compliance with this requirement. SCAMPI stands for Standard CMMI based Appraisal Method for Process Improvement. SCAMPI has 3 types of Appraisals in it.

SCAMPI C – The lightest method, the appraisals can be based on artifacts or Oral affirmation. The purpose of this appraisal method is quickly to understand the high level approach issues and interpretation issues. We need a Team Leader certified by CMMI Institute to do the SCAMPI C appraisal. This is not mandatory activity, if you are looking for achieving a particular maturity rating. However it's preferred to have this kind of appraisal for early correction in approach.

SCAMPI B – The method helps to understand in detail the weakness and strength in process areas. We can adopt this when we are in mid stage of implementation or in 75% progress in our journey. The missing elements can be identified and it gives deeper understanding. Cost wise this is lesser costlier than SCAMPI A. We need certified Team Leader for SCAMPI B appraisal to conduct this appraisal. We need a team of members to participate along with team leader to perform appraisal. If we have Appraisal Team Members (trained), it will be added advantage. This is again not mandatory, but definitely recommended to avoid any surprise.

SCAMPI A – The only method which meets all the requirements of ARC and which can produce results in terms of "Rating" at organizational level is this method. To perform this we need a Certified Lead Appraiser (Up to ML3) or a Certified High Maturity Lead Appraiser (Up to ML5) and team of trained members in CMMI Model and in Appraisal Methodology. The Results provided this method is valid for 3 years and the sponsor of the program can select publishing it in PARS site of CMMI Institute, where your results based on confidentiality chosen will be available for external world to view. It's a very detailed method and multiple analysis method is available like a) Verification method b) Discovery method and c) Managed Discovery Method. Most of them like to go with Managed Discovery method, where they collect minimum required information before appraisal and take the discovery approach to better understand the implementation. This greatly reduced the level of effort put in PIID (Process Implementation Indicator Document) preparation.

For more understanding on SCAMPI Method, you can download MDD (Method Definition Document) from CMMIInstitute.com

Appraisal Phase Activities:

a) Appraisal Scope Discussion: Before you enter this phase, it's expected that the Lead Appraiser is already identified and formal introduction about your organization and a meeting with sponsor should have been done. In this activity it's important to discuss with him on the appraisal scope you are looking forward and define them clearly in a word document. This could be the one in later point of time, submitted in CMMI Institute Appraisal System (SAS) and may come in the Appraisal plan document. The terminologies shall be at industry standard and which your client can understand. Similarly discuss with lead appraiser on units to be included and projects which are falling under the scope of appraisal. Organizational unit is the terminology which defines the boundary of the organization which has implemented the model and to be included in appraisal. It can happen that only one production/service line you have considered in Implementation and then organizational unit is only inclusive of that line. Once you and the lead appraiser has come in to understanding, by this time, you will also have collected some idea from your lead appraiser that how he/she is planning to select the projects or samples for the given condition.

The SCAMPI v1.3 method contains sample case for the Organizations to understand the sampling. The key is finding the factors which introduce variation in implementation and create distinct sample groups out of them. Then based out of overall work units in the Organizational unit and the number of work unit in each distinctive sample group, the ratio are derived and the final number of sample work unit to be looked in appraisal is derived using the pre defined formula in the method. The simple clue you can take is , the lesser the variation and more or less equal number within in the sample groups, then you will end with less work units to look in to appraisal. This means less cost and typical normal schedule.

Sampling of Sub groups – with three varying factors (site, Domain, Type)						
	Site	Domain	Type	Basic Units	Sample Calc	Sample Size
Sub Group1	Paris	Banking	Implementation	20	1.5	2
Sub	Paris	Healthcare	Upgrade	4	0.3	1

Group2						
Sub Group3	Paris	Manufacturing	Implementation	2	0.1	1
Sub Group4	Beijing	Banking	Implementation	40	3.0	3
Sub Group5	Beijing	Manufacturing	Implementation	1	0.1	1
Total 5				Total67		

The Formula application for sample size of Basic units from each sub group is (Total number of sub groups/ Total Basic Units) * Basic units in that sub group. In this case sub group 1 sample size is (5/67)*20 = 1.5 => 2, similarly others are also calculated.

b) Appraisal Team Member Selection: The appraisal members are selected typically nearer to the last quarter to ensure their stay in the organization for the period is confirmed. The Appraisal team members should have certain qualifications in terms of experience in technical and project management side, reporting clearance and competency. The expectations are set clear in the new method, and the lead appraiser will discuss with organization and will ensure the requirements are met. From organization's point of view, you may need your best people or the practitioner to sit as Functional Area Representative (FAR) than as Appraisal Team Member (ATM). However you may need to have few people from your Process QA Group to be there, so process related doubts and working methods can be explained well. For smaller organizations who don't have many , they can take external ATM's or can declare the conflicts about a person representing the ATM team, that can be planned and managed by Lead Appraiser. It's always a good practice to bring few external ATM's to get better objective results.

However it also has slight risk on not understanding the context on timely manner.

Appraisal Team Members shall undergo formal "CMMI Introduction" training for the respective model which is planned to be appraised in your organization. If you go for combined appraisal, then CMMI Dev + CMMI Svc addition training is required or you can send them for training on both the method separately. This training can be provided only by a Certified CMMI Instructor, your lead appraiser may have this certification, so he can do this. The trained member names, dates of training and organizational name is collected and send to CMMI Institute, normally within weeks it's added to their records. This is important for the members to be part of Appraisal, because the SAS will have to show their record to the lead appraiser to add in to a newly created appraisal as Appraisal Team Member. The "Official Introduction to CMMI- Dev/Svc" can be a separate program planned for your organization or shared program with organizations or regular planned public programs conducted by the CMMI Instructors. This is of 3 days duration and at the end you will receive a certificate of training with CMMI Institute emblem.

Appraisal Team training is provided by the Lead Appraiser of the appraisal. If you have already just participated in an appraisal for the same constellation as team member, the lead appraiser may chose not to give you the training but to include you as team member. CMMI Institute never gives any certificate for this role, if at all it's given; it's normally by the CMMI Partner. However in the ATM pool database in SAS (appraisal system- portal) the names of eligible people to participate in an appraisal for a constellation is listed by their training record. The ATM training is of 2 days duration and normally lead appraiser's combined them with SCAMPI B or Readiness Review, which gives the ATM's better understanding on applying the SCAMPI practices and getting ready for SCAMPI A. There is a simple open book pre qualifying test too.

c) Appraisal Plan: Appraisal plan is prepared by the lead appraiser based on the various inputs collected in the organization to schedule the SCAMPI A appraisal. The scope, sampling, resources to be involved, plan for data collection, details on appraisal onsite schedule, Appraisal Team Member details, back ground on the organization and other details are documented in this. The Appraisal Plan normally undergoes multiple iterations to ensure accuracy and updated details. The Sponsor from your organization and Lead Appraiser have to sign the document. The Appraisal Team Member sign is also taken on this. Appraisal plan should be agreed before getting in to SCAMPI A onsite period.

Data collection activities have to be planned in every appraisal and these details are submitted to CMMI Institute. With many of them moving to Managed Discovery Approach, the huge exercise of PIID preparation is no longer a concern in the new SCAMPI V1.3 Method. The Important Artifacts which covers most of the practices and acts as evidence is collected and stored in relevant places. The Appraisal teams are given with relevant hints and they are able to locate and tag them in readiness review and they raise documents request to the internal teams. Based on the responses, the relevant documents are added to their evaluation system. In a sense the appraisal teams have to be a bit smarter, however this has reduced the workload a lot.

d) Readiness Review: The Readiness in terms of Infrastructure, access needs, artifact availability and others are checked in this activity. Normally a target of 80 to 90% is set by Lead Appraisers. There is a time limit of gap between Readiness Review and SCAMPI A appraisal is there. Similarly the Overall SCAMPI A cycle is to be completed within 90 days.

e) Preparation for SCAMPI A: It's very normal that Organizations give some level understanding to the FAR group members on how to approach an appraisal. This is in one way helps the Appraisal activity, as totally out of context talks don't happen and better utilization of interview time. However giving training on what to talk or rehearsal on how to deliver can be avoided, as that's not the intent of interview. The FAR group member should communicate the actual and appraisal team members, basically listen and notes down the facts given by them.

f) SCAMPI A Onsite Activity: Ensure that Sponsor, FAR group members and support teams are available, apart from your ATM's availability. Ensure that relevant logistics, infrastructure teams are available for the support. The onsite coordinator is responsible for ensuring all the relevant logistics available and right communication happens with organization. Participation in Opening meeting, Preliminary findings and final findings could be the three meetings the FAR group members to attend apart from their scheduled Interview.

The Appraisal Team collects the facts from oral affirmation (Interviews) and checks the Artifacts supporting the practices. Then the findings are documented. With that information the rating generation happens. Before they generate practices, goals, and PA and Organizational Level ratings the team presents the findings to the FAR group members and gets their views, where the FAR group members believe they have additional information which the ATM's to look, that's been submitted. The entire Appraisal Team activities are guided and managed by the Lead Appraiser, the lesser the disturbance given to them, more the efficiency will result. Finally the final findings are presented. It's the sponsor who has to decide, whether he/she wants everyone to be present or not as audience for this presentation, as only he/she is the entitled one.

All the artifacts created in the process have to be distinguished and the copies which have to be retained are well managed by the Lead Appraisers and others are destroyed.

The Lead Appraiser submits the results in the CMMI Appraisal System. Normally the CMMI Institute team looks at the appraisal plan and the relevant details provided to them and verify it. In some cases, the appraisal might be taken for Audit by SCAMPI Quality team and they ask for further information on the appraisal process to the Lead appraiser. Once the data is validated by them the audit process is cleared then your results will be published in the CMMI Institute PARS site, in case if it's not selected for audit, the results will be published as soon as in CMMI Institute PARS site. The sponsor is kept informed in all the happenings by the CMMI Institute along with the Lead Appraiser.

Once you get your results in CMMI PARS it's time to go for celebration and be proud of the system you have created in your Organization!

SUSTAINING CMMI IMPLEMENTATION

Sustenance Phase in CMMI is assumed to be the normal life in organization. If you have implemented CMMI well, by this time that's your normal process and way of working and you have nothing to do in addition. The only roles which may disappear soon after CMMI rating achievement is CMMI program manager and steering committee specifically set up to reach the target. The other things which you need to take care is,

- Do not dilute your Process QA group and not to reduce the strength

- Do not modify the SEPG

- Improvements should be your next course of action

- Improve the effectiveness of Audits

- Make an yearly appraisal plan with SEPG for your processes

- Keep conducting meetings with senior management from process point of view

- Do necessary evaluation based on CMMI on any new additional services added in your QMS

- Keep Evaluating your business needs

- Ensure your policies kept up to date

- Bring in an award and appreciation mechanism to project teams on better compliance

- Perform QMS Gap Analysis on regular basis

- Process QA group can concentrate on effectiveness of audits and facilitation

- Your communication channels can be used for appreciation of good performance

- Continue Monthly newsletters as informative and community networking tool

- Important to address all the recommendations given in SCAMPI A

CMMI HIGH MATURITY IMPLEMENTATION

CMMI High Maturity denotes the Maturity level 4 and 5, considering Organization needs to put additional effort and improve their competency with people, process and technology to reach these levels. Also the organizations achieve capability to find and eliminate in effective tasks/components in processes and bring in effective and efficient replacement components to achieve Business results, and all of these with well informed and applied quantitative techniques.

Considering High Maturity Practices needs detailed understanding and relevant application of techniques, this book would deal the High maturity practices only at concept level. We would recommend attending CMMI Institute courses or taking the help of good SME/Consultant to have better understanding on this.

What is High Maturity?

- Setting business & project goals

- Understand the past performance of standard and defined processes

- Develop prediction models and estimate / predict future performance of standard and defined processes

- Manage project (Project Defined Process) using past performance and future predictions

- Take appropriate corrections (either at the beginning / at different phases) towards meeting goals

- Bring continuous improvements / innovations into processes, tools and technology to meet business goals

- Develop highest potential from people, tools and technology

The following are considered to be Important in high maturity implementation,

a) Timeline: Organizations has to be already there in CMMI Maturity Level 3 to reach High Maturity Levels. This is not a mandate, but practically when you operate with standard set of processes; it would be easier for you to go the next maturity level. Remember the Maturity level can't be skipped, which means, even you go for rating or not, you must have applied all the relevant applicable processes till the level you are looking forward. Hence Maturity Level 3 is a good plateau from where you can improve your processes to next maturity level. Typically you should plan minimum of 2 year road map for your High Maturity. Its normal not only the community but even CMMI Institute will look at your Maturity with surprise if you achieve your high maturity within a year from your CMMI ML3. It's practical to suspect, because the time required implementing the quantitative practice, getting data from them, improving based on them and meeting the business goals actually needs a logical time period of minimum 2 years. Data points are not a concern here, let the organization has as much as data point, but the stability cycle and improvement cycle needs time.

b) People Competency: Definitely you may need to ensure that the people also have relevant competency to accept these high maturity processes and techniques. Typically we would expect the project managers to have competency not only in project management but also in relevant Quantitative and Statistical techniques. The Project managers shall be able to understand their data/results and apply relevant techniques and interpret them accordingly to take decisions. Similarly the Causal analysis and QC tools understanding are required. Sometime in Lower maturity levels, organizations can survive with project managers who really don't understand the measures or has less authority to take project decision, but in High Maturity levels we believe the project managers is self sufficient in terms of interpreting and taking decisions of quantitative results. Similarly the metrics group shall be trained in statistical methods and Process QA Group should be aware of Process performance models and their application. The Process QA group normally assists the project managers, hence they should be aware of basic statistics to perform the job. Even the management team should have understanding on basic statistics.

c) Tools: The High Maturity levels need better maturity in terms of tools also. Typically the data need for analysis purpose of various process is priority. Hence if you have a poor timesheet tool, scheduling tool, defect management tool, etc. you may face problem. We have to understand the base measures most of the time revolves around effort, time and defect. When we don't have precise data on them but the system has pre exist bias reporting, then those will not help in High Maturity. Improve the tools to ensure that precise and accurate data can be collected. Improve the process where required to increase the accuracy. In addition to these you may need statistical analysis tool and modeling tools. There are so many different tools available in the market, some of them free, some we can make with macros, and some are available for cost. Statistical tools like Minitab, Sigma XL, JMP and others are widely used by organizations. Floating/concurrent licenses are one way to reduce your cost in tools. Similarly for simulation purpose some of them create Excel based macros and some use tool like crystal ball. Most of the tools mentioned here can help you Process Performance Modeling (Like regression model, simulation, and Design of Experiments and Reliability models) and there are special tools available for process modeling and discrete event simulation methods (Processmodel tool) and for dynamic modeling. You have to spend time and energy to decide which one will be the best one for your case.

d) Process: The Process in the organization will undergo changes for betterment, not only new processes will be written, even the existing processes will be re evaluated for better clarity and ensure distinctive and accurate measures can be established with the process. If you already have project management process, you may be interested in looking at your estimation process and planning process in detail. To some extent we are talking on sub process here, but more than that clarity is required in the tasks and most of them should be measurable. The new processes will be written to bring in the new process area practices to implementation. The new practices at high maturity level helps your engineering/services and support processes to stabilize and to improve their capability. Organizations can write these processes on their own or where required they can check with their consultant to write these processes. We would recommend writing on their own with understanding clarity established with their consultant.

e) Consulting and Review Needs: You may need a SME or Consultant to help in you in few areas when it comes to High Maturity. A consultant is required for providing clarification on High Maturity practices, Process Capability Baseline preparation, process performance model preparation and Review on Causal Analysis activities. In addition to this you may need them to check the implementation of high maturity practices. Information required for high maturity is mostly available in CMMI Institute release presentations, and information like Business objectives fixing, QPM/QWM interpretations are mostly available. In addition CMMI Institute also conducts High Maturity Training, which is more useful in implementation.

High Maturity Process Areas Quick Look:

Organizational process Performance (ML4):

Before we look in to the practices of this process area, it's important for your organization to have clear business objectives and as far as possible, keep them SMART (Specific, Measurable, Attainable, Relevant and Time bound) objective.

Sample Business Objective:

By Jul 2014, Organization will improve Customer Satisfaction from today's baseline of mean 7.2 and Standard Deviation 2.2 to a new baseline of mean 7.5 and Standard deviation 1.5 with 95% confidence without sacrificing Profit Margin.

The usage of Mean is based should be after confirming the data is having Normal Distribution, for non normal data follow Median.

SP1.1 Establish and maintain the organization's quantitative objectives for quality and Process performance, which are traceable to business objectives.

Brief: The factors which are affecting the business objectives are identified. Their relationship with Business Objectives is verified with data. On Confirmation of the relationship, the Quality and Process performance objectives are defined. Quality objectives are given to emphasize the importance of quality parameters.

In this case for example Customer Satisfaction is there, which could be analyzed with multiple factors in the development a) Effort b) schedule c) Resource competency d) Defects e) first time right, etc on Services a) SLA compliance b) Resource Competency c) Back log index d) Change

Request clearance index ,etc

You can use simple technique like correlation study and regression analysis to understand the relationship with Business objective. Based on the identified factor which influences the Business objective, defined the Quality and Process Performance Objective (QPPO).

Sample QPPO:

By end of 2013, Organization will reduce effort variance from mean 14.5 and S.D 2.5 to a new baseline of mean 11 and S.D 2.5 with 95% confidence without increasing Defect density

By end of 2013, Organization will improve SLA compliance from mean 92 and S.D 3 to a new baseline of mean 95 and S.D 2 with 95% confidence without increasing Defect density

SP1.2: Select processes or sub processes in the organizations set of processes to be included in the organizations process performance analysis and maintain traceability to business objectives

Brief: Identify the processes or sub process which are having direct relationship with QPPO and B.O and where required having the data based analysis will help. On the other hand when you have process performance models, which contains factors coming out of your processes and sub processes they will become the one which you may want to include in analysis.

Example: Analysis, design, coding and testing processes directly contributes to Effort variance, on the other hand competency management process may have influence on the same (established in process performance model), and so you may include all of them in process capability baseline.

Similarly the incident management process by priority and service request process influence the SLA compliance. Also the sub process like analyze, develop, test and fix sub processes can also be influencing the SLA compliance in certain priority. Hence they also may be selected for analysis. Typically the process performance model or specific relationship models are established to prove the traceability in quantitative manner.

SP1.3: Establish and Maintain definitions of Measures to be included in the Organizations process performance analysis

Brief: The measures has to be clearly defined with units, collection period, clarity in source, role, analysis details, usage of QC tools for analysis, guideline on how to interpret and for Metrics the formula for calculation has to be defined. The scale usage for the measure help in determining the relevant statistical analysis tests to be performed.

In this case on Effort, we have analysis, design, coding, testing all these processes will have measure on Effort normalized with the unit size produced. The measure of effort and relevant details can be given in a common definition document.

Similarly the time taken for analyze, develop, test and fix sub processes will have measures like cycle time which might be the influencing factor in the process performance model for the QPPO identified.

SP1.4: Analyze the performance of the selected processes, and establish and maintain the process performance baselines.

Brief: Process Performance baselines are derived from project data. Process Performance analyzes are derived by analyzing the collected measures to establish a distribution and range results that characterize the expected performance for selected processes when used on any individual project in the organization.

The PPB helps in,

- Establish and verify the reasonableness of organizational and Project objectives

- Compose the project defined processes

- Establish Trail limits

- Identify potential sources of problems for Outcome Analysis

- Identify opportunities for improvement

- Evaluate the effect of changes after pilot or improvement

PPB's are based on data available on frequent enough rate and timely fashion, based on common measures defined in the organization, it contains time ordered data and non time ordered data, it addresses all Processes and sub processes measures selected, it can have stable process data and Non stable process data (indicate them appropriately). The PPB's also contains the analysis of measures and corrective action details to be taken to improve the performance.

The following are typically the checks performed on Measures reported in PPB,

a) Check the data for accuracy and precision

b) Performing Gauge R&R will help in ensuring data quality

c) Box Plot and verify the data for variations

d) Check the data for Normality

e) Perform Stability check on data (western electric rule or 8 point check)

f) Perform data outlier analysis

g) Process capability can be determined Cp and Cpk

h) Establish Graphical Distribution analysis – Mean, S.D , Quartiles, median, Control limits, others

i) Hypothesis testing (where required to prove, change in central tendency or variation) –with parametric test (Normal distribution) and Non Parametric test (Non Normal distribution) are performed

Typically, the PPB has all the relevant measures and compares it with previous PPB and indicates if there is any change in Central tendency and variation and trend details apart from the measures.

In addition to that establish trend analysis for the QPPO.

The following could be the contents in your PPB,

1) Process Performance baseline overview

    a. Process Performance baseline objective

    b. Process Performance baseline scope

2) Definition, Acronyms and Abbreviations

3) List of Project Buckets

4) Segmentation and Stratification

5) List of Process and sub process measures

6) Current Goals and Objectives

7) Process performance baseline summary

    a. Change in projects

    b. Changes in Project Baseline and Goals

8) Graphical Summary and Analysis for Each Measure

9) Causal Analysis

10) Recommendations

11) Assumptions

12) Annexure

Key steps in Process Performance baseline preparation are,

- Collect and analyze measurement data from projects

- Establish and maintain Organizational process performance baseline from the collected measurement data, using the steps given above

- Review and get agreement with all relevant stakeholders about the process performance baselines

- Publish your process performance baselines to the members in organization

- Compare the baselines and associated business objectives and plan for improvements

- Revise the Process Performance baselines as necessary (new service lines, significant changes, process changes, improvements, etc)

Typically a Central Metrics/Statistical Process control team involves in preparation of PPB and it gets discussed in SEPG and final approval comes from SEPG Head for release.

Tools like Minitab, sigma XL, MS Excel with Macros, JMP and others can be used for making the PPB. Some organizations use word format, some uses Excel and some uses web pages.

SP1.5: Establish and Maintain process performance models for the organization's set of standard processes.

Processes Performance Models (PPM) s is used to predict the value of a process performance measure from the values of other process and product/service measurements. PPM's typically use process and product/service measurements collected throughout the lifecycle to estimate progress towards achieving objectives, which can't be measured until later in lifecycle.

These models typically let us know the critical processes which are influencing the business objective significantly. The result of PPM is an interval (prediction interval) than a single point prediction (that's why earned value analysis is not a PPM).

These ranges typically help us to understand the probability of achieving results at project level, when used in projects. Typically the PPMs are based on static data (past performance) and few PPMs are based on dynamic data (the relationship of model established with live data). Static models like multiple regression, dummy variable regression are popular in community and similarly reliability growth model is an example of dynamic model.

How PPM's are used,

- Establish and verify meeting of Business Objectives or Project Objectives , hence reasonability is verified

- Determine the project progress to meet final objectives

- Analyze, impact and predict the benefit of

  o Outcome analysis corrective actions

  o Action proposal for improvements

  o Innovations proposed

  o Corrective actions aimed at improving critical process

- Evaluate the proposed change in terms of predictable results

Essential Ingredients of Process Performance Model are,

- Model should relate behavior of a process or sub process to an outcome (QPPO)

- The Model should be able to predict outcomes based on possible changes to the factors (support what if analysis)

- The model uses factors of sub process or process to conduct the prediction. When more of controllable factors are figuring in that, we have more chance of controlling the final outcome; however it can have uncontrollable factors also to represent the reality.

- The models are statistical or probabilistic in nature, which accounts variation, rather than deterministic

- It could be collection of models which predicts outcome of Interest

Few Types of Modelling:

- Statistical Models – Multiple Regression, Dummy variable Regression, logistic , Log Normal regression and many

- Monte Carlo simulation models

- Process Simulation – Using computerized simulation

- Discrete Event Simulation

- Discrete Event Simulation with Queuing theory

- Reliability growth

- Neural network and many more

Process Performance Models can be generated first with a good overall system flow and by clearly noting the processes which are contributing to it. Then identify the factors which influence each of these processes. With this understanding the relevant data can be collected and their relationship with the final outcome can be studied. If there is positive or negative relationship they can be noted down. Select those factors of processes which have significant relationship (many cases correlation co-efficient helps) and feed them in to the model which are designing. Construct the model and see whether the results show relevant relationship of factors with Outcome. Where required, change the factors combination and try again. The best possible relationship model together and every individual factor distinctively contribute to the prediction and not hindered by other factors, will create a good model. Where the model results are not statistically verifiable, then use the actual data and see the prediction results and compare the allowable prediction variation.

In our case, if we are looking forward to effort variance at project level then Analysis, design, coding and testing process effort (normalized with size) might have relationship, similarly the factors impacting the processes also might have relationship, example - Complexity of design, stability in requirements, coverage in testing, customer type, competency of Business Analyst, test case number and so on (there can be many). However you have to narrow down the factors, first by analyzing with your team and finding the causes using fishbone, and then collect data on them to verify. The factors we gave earlier some of them are controllable and some of them are non controllable (ex: Customer Type), however your model can have both. Also based on type of data (discrete or continuous) the modeling technique and tools can differ.

Assume that we use regression model and it's based on continuous data, you may do correlation analysis with each factor and Effort variance and then select the ones which has significance and add it to Multiple Regression Analysis (you may be using Minitab, Sigma XL, R, JMP or any tool) and might achieve a better relationship equation like

Effort Variance (Y) = 0.25 * Complexity of Design (X1) + 0.51*Req. Stability (X2) – 1.2 * Coverage in Testing

Normally we will go with R2 adjusted value (more than 80%) and then study the individual relationship with factors, then look at F statistic (or) P value which should be less than 0.05 (if 95% C.I) to prove that at least one of the factor influence the Outcome (Y). Not only this, you need to see the standard residual and other parameters before concluding.

Similarly, in a dynamic model like process modeling the model is constructed with process flow with each and every step (sub process) and decision loops. The data on these sub processes are collected and factor influencing them (like complexity, competency level, etc) are configured and the model is run with simulation. The running length is typically the period like a day/ week or month which you are trying to check with outcome. Remember when you are feeding in the data, you feed the range based on actual distribution model of data of these factors. The final result is the predicted outcome. However in this model, the model can be validated only be checking a particular period actual data and check the deviation of predicted outcome and actual outcome. As long as the deviation is within the range (risk accepted by organization) the model can be used in organization.

The PPM's are revised when, there is change in any process, when improvement actions performed, significant change in any of the process measure or factor.

Quantitative Project/Work Management:

SP1.1: Establish and Maintain projects' quality and process performance objectives

Brief: Consider the Organizations' QPPO and Client given objectives, based on that derive the first level project objectives, Cross check the Process performance baseline in the organization and use the process performance model with trail values and see whether the Project objectives are achievable. Negotiate the project objectives if required.

Sample: Effort variance in the project should be lesser than 10% with 95% confidence level

SLA compliance should be greater than 95% with 95% confidence level

SP1.2: Using Statistical and other quantitative techniques, compose a defined process that enables the work to achieve its quality and process performance objectives

Brief: Typically the process performance model which you use is having all the relevant process in the lifecycle connected. Also we believe the project objectives are predictable by one or more PPM you have developed (in combination). In such a case, the process performance model is run with relevant simulation with identified process/sub process and what if analysis are performed by varying the process values (by depth variation or adjustment in tasks), similarly the alternate processes have been checked with their values in the final prediction. The composition of process/sub process which gives lesser risk in the probability of achieving the expected project objectives (using PPM) is selected for further analysis and monitoring and those processes are formalized for execution in Project.

Tools like Crystal ball, JMP, Process Model and other simulation enabled tools can help in performing this practice and learn the probability level/certainty level with relevant process composition. Obviously we might want a probability of more than 95%, and otherwise we have to consider the risk and make a plan to mitigate or accept it.

SP1.3: Select sub processes and attributes critical to evaluating performance and that help to achieve the quality and process performance objectives for the work.

Brief: The Sub Processes which are critical to achieve the QPPO can be selected based on a) The major contributors and predictors to the achievement of the projects objectives b) The subset of the organizationally selected processes and sub-processes c) The processes and sub processes reflected in the organizational baselines and models d) Also the sub process provides sufficient data for monitoring and control.

The sub processes which are part of the PPM will be considered in addition to this, and basically we try to stabilize these processes or alter the performance level so that the project objectives can be achieved.

In our sample case, we will select the sub process like Analyze, design, design review, code review and others. Please note that design review or code review can be sub process. We would recommend following the terminology description given for "Sub process" in CMMI Model. Similarly in services where you are trying to achieve SLA compliance as objectives, Priority 1 sub process, Priority 2 sub process, priority 3 analyze sub process, priority 3 develop sub process, etc can be the sub process (Incident management is considered as process in this case). These sub processes in our case, we assume has significance in final outcome/project objectives, and the same can be proven with our performance models or statistical relationships (don't' miss out logical relationship).

SP1.4: Select Measures and analytic techniques to be used in quantitative management

Each critical sub processes and its related measures of interest is selected for quantitative management and similarly the analytic techniques are identified for those measures. The techniques like Scatter plots, control charts, run chart, Box plot, Pareto chart, histogram, Hypothesis test (T test, ANOVA, Kruskal Wallis, Chi-square test, etc) are identified for the purpose.

Example: Code Review sub process, we may measure productivity/effort per unit and IMR chart could be the analysis technique we may use. Similarly Priority 3 develop sub process (Incident Management) may have measure cycle time and IMR chart may be the analysis technique used.

SP2.1: Monitor the performance of selected sub processes using statistical and other quantitative techniques

The selected sub process are monitored based on the pre identified frequency (it depends on the execution of sub process), where the sub process is executed on daily basis a monitoring on daily or weekly could be more meaningful. The importance is, to understand the behavior of sub process and control the special causes, and when there is shift in process based on planned changes be aware and monitor them for changes.

Mostly control charts are used to monitor the stability of process (selection of control charts should be based on type of data) and any special cause is analyzed and corrective actions are taken. In our case, when code review has taken more time in a particular case (out of range), then analyzes performed and corrective action applied. At the beginning trail limits from PPB might be taken, as more the data comes from the sub process the natural limits for the sub process is established.

Example: Code review effort control limits are 0.75 to 1.5 hrs per unit code, in a special case, if the outlier goes beyond 1.5 hrs or lesser than 0.75 its analyzed for special cause. Similarly if any trend is seen in the data plots (perform 8 point stability check/western electric rule) then analysis performed and sub process is notified as instable.

SP2.2: Manage the work using statistical and other quantitative techniques to determine whether or not the quality and process performance objectives for the work/project will be satisfied

The process performance model is used at the beginning of each identified phase/month/milestones or any identified frequency to understand the probability of achieving the project objective. When the predicted values are deviated much or certainty level is low, causal analysis can be triggered to address the factors. Similarly in the middle of lifecycle on all the relevant milestones or in intermediate points the PPM can be used to predict the Project objectives. Remember to manage all the project objectives and in case of prioritization of project objectives, you can manage them using relevant PPM, however it's important to verify no other project objectives are compromised.

In the case where we have taken Effort variance, at the beginning of every phase the PPM can be run with the actual data available till that phase and further phases with variation and simulation can be done to predict the values. Similarly in case of SLA compliance, beginning of the month and middle of the month the PPM can be run with the actual values of the attributes of the process.

Where the project objectives are not going to meet, apply corrective actions and bring in causal analysis as required.

SP2.3: Perform root cause analysis of selected issues to address deficiencies in achieving the work group's /projects quality process performance objectives

The causal analyses are triggered whenever there is potential issue that project objectives are not met or reactively looking at the actual on QPPO. The root causes are identified normally using fishbone diagram or other technique and the corrective actions are identified. The actions are tracked to closure, where required cost benefit analysis can be performed.

The change in performance is monitored and where required PPM is used to predict the Project objectives.

In the case of effort variance, where consistently the code reviews have taken higher effort and/or the PPM is predicting high Effort variance, root cause analysis can be performed and relevant root cause identified, eliminated with corrective action, then the PPM can be re run with the new values of the factor. Similarly when we understand that SLA compliance is predicted to be on lower range for that period, root cause analysis can be triggered and corrective actions can be taken.

Causal Analysis and Resolution (ML5):

SP1.1 Select Outcome for Analysis:

Outcome here refers to any value of our interest in project level. Typically the project objectives which we want to attain can be Outcomes for analysis, however it doesn't limit only to them. Considering this is supportive process area the intent is to apply to any outcome.

PPB and PPM's can be useful in identifying the outcomes which can be considered for analysis. Consider the impact of the outcome, frequency of happening, cost of the analysis, ROI and time it will take, while selecting the outcome for analysis.

In our case, you can take effort variance which will not meet as per the prediction and SLA for a month which will not meet can be taken for analysis.

SP1.2: Perform Causal Analysis of selected outcomes and propose actions to address them

Organizations sometime have special teams to coordinate the causal analysis activities at organizational level and at project level. This is purely depends on the need of the context and the kind of outcomes the organization has to address and how the organizational structure is, people availability, etc. Typically a good analysis of data and simple techniques like Pareto chart and fish bone diagram application can help in identifying the qualitative root causes. With adequate data the causes can be identified and corrective actions can be taken.

SP2.1: Implement selected action proposals developed in causal analysis

The action proposal coming out of causal analysis can be evaluated with ROI, PPM usage to see if the action items are useful to apply and bring improvement in the outcome. Application of PPM and cost benefit analysis would help in getting the better action proposals.

SP2.2: Evaluate the effect of Implemented actions on Process Performance

As the corrective actions are identified, they are tracked to closure. Their effect on the process performance shall be checked using quantitative and/or statistical techniques. Application of hypothesis testing on the results of outcome before and after change helps to confirm the effect of implemented action. The other techniques used are box plot and control charts; they help us to understand the significant changes in the process or Project objectives.

In the case of effort variance, an action taken to implement automated code review tool, how much it has changed the process performance of code review can be checked with box plot and stability understanding with control chart. Also the Hypothesis testing of before and after data will help in proving that they both are not same. Similarly reducing the time of analysis process of incident management by having knowledge data base could be the solution and its effect can be checked with relevant techniques.

SP2.3: Record Causal analysis and resolution data for use across work groups and the organization

Ensuring the actions are applied and the records are stored for use for others and availability of the solution across work groups (projects) helps in improving the system.

In this case the automated code review tool implementation across organization or implementing a Knowledge data base across Organization, which are solutions identified from causal analysis can be deployed with use of SEPG.

Organization Performance Management (ML5)

SP1.1: Maintain business objectives based on an understanding of business strategies and actual performance results

Brief: The organizational business objectives are established in SMART format already. Here we are trying to maintain the business objectives using any change in business strategies (new business line, change in service, etc) and looking at how good we are progressing on actual performance in terms of business objective. Trend Analysis of business objectives will provide details on how good we are progressing towards meeting business objectives. Similarly look at the QPPO's and compare the actual and revise them as necessary.

A revision of Business and/ or QPPO with relevant data or comparison of targeted objectives with actual values/ trend would help in this.

SP1.2: Analyze Process performance data to determine the Organization's ability to meet identified business objectives

Brief: Considering that we are developing process performance baselines on periodically, the process performance data coming out these PPB's can be used to determine, whether the business objectives will be achieved. The QPPOs are compared with the current PPB to evaluate whether the B.O can be achieved. Wherever there is risk of not meeting the objectives that can be documented and improvements can be planned.

In our case, when we understand that we have code review effort operating at some level, which leads to certain range of Effort variance (using PPM) and for that range the customer satisfaction range can be predicted. Similarly the SLA compliance level is lower (in current PPB) than the targeted one, this could be further analyzed for the risks.

SP1.3: Identify potential areas for improvement that could contribute to meeting business objectives

Brief: The potential areas for improvement can be identified using, shortfalls in not meeting the process objectives or process capability issues. These could be the indicators that a particular area needs improvement. In addition Causal Analysis technique can help us to determine them.

These potential areas can be evaluated for cost benefit and can be taken for further evaluation and prioritization.

In the case we have taken, If the design process is taking higher effort or injecting more defects, then it could be a potential area to look at (with data, do analysis including Pareto and fishbone, check variation, predict the impact) and improve. Perform cost benefit analysis, by understanding to what extent actually it would improve the QPPO and by that Business Objective. The same way, the Test process in P3 incident ticket if it's a concern that it takes more time (less resource /more volume/improper code completion information/poor quality code), thereby increases queue. This could be a potential area for improvement, again use the relevant tools to diagnose it.

SP2.1: Elicit and Categorize suggested Improvement

Brief: Elicit the improvements in an area through various sources (Improvement log, Technical portals, contests, process appraisal, client feedback, others) and analyze them for their expected benefit. Categorize the improvements as Innovative (expected to make shift in performance or reduce the variation to good extent) or Incremental Improvements (gradual improvement in performance).

Investigate whether these improvements will make changes in processes and technologies.

SP2.2: Analyze suggested improvements for their possible impact on achieving the organization's quality and process performance objectives

Brief: Analyze the improvements using cost benefit method and see whether they can be really effective. Check how to validate the improvement before deploying them throughout.

In our case, if we try to bring in a Design Architecture validation tool, which can reduce poor designing. Then we would like to evaluate, will this really work and what could be the cost and benefit of this.

SP2.3: Validate Selected Improvements

Brief: Where required plan for piloting and have a validation method. The validation method should be based on the actual values the improvement could achieve. Perform hypothesis testing as required to see, if the improvement has made effect in the final outcome.

In our case, if we have implemented the Design architecture tool in selected projects and have seen improvement in terms better design quality and less design review effort that can be checked with hypothesis testing. The same way, assume that we have implemented test automation tool for P3 priority incidents and has automated test scripts to test similar incidents, then the results improvement achieved with this implementation can be validated with hypothesis test.

SP2.4: Select and Implement improvements for deployment throughout the organization based on an evaluation of costs, benefits and other factors

Brief: Once we decide with validation, that a particular improvement will help in achieving the objectives, and then it's evaluated with costs, benefits and deploy ability (need in different units, resources, method, technology, communication, etc). If the evaluation results are good, then the improvement is selected for deployment in the organization. Remember we do the evaluation at the beginning on improvement area and to consider a improvement for implementation and validation. Not all the validated improvements may go for deployment, because the condition could differ. Hence again we do cost benefit analysis here.

SP3.1: Establish and maintain plans for deploying selected improvements

Brief: We make deployment plan to ensure all the relevant projects/work units can deploy the improvement. Deployment plan includes training plan, schedule, strategy of implementation, effort required, QMS release/process updates, Resource required, effectiveness checking, etc. The deployment plan made at the beginnings shall be kept up to date, based on the feedback or status. The schedule might undergo changes based on the kind of issues/barriers faced in deployment or support required. Hence maintain the deployment plan.

SP3.2: Manage deployment of selected improvements

Brief: The deployment is supported with resources and the plan is executed. During the course of deployment the trainings are executed, processes released, projects are added to the umbrella and many more. Hence effective tracking and corrective actions are required. At the end of deployment its expected as per the original plan (/revised) you were able to deploy the improvements and records are available

SP3.3: Evaluate the effects of deployed Improvements on Quality and Process Performance using statistical and other quantitative techniques

Brief: As the deployment happens, the PPM can be used to predict the QPPO meeting target. As the deployment is complete, we could use techniques like hypothesis testing to validate if there is any change (ex: compare the previous and current PPB values) and also we can use PPM to see the probability of meeting QPPOs.

AGILE WITH CMMI & ALTERNATE PRACTICES

Agile with CMMI mapping:

The following table contains mapping for CMMI when we execute agile projects. These are again typical artifacts and would vary from organization to organization. We would request you to evaluate accordingly.

Process Area- Specific Goals & Specific Practices	Agile Scrum Artifacts
Requirements Management	
SG 1 Manage Requirements	
SP 1.1 Understand Requirements	Product backlog
SP 1.2 Obtain Commitment to Requirements	Release planning meeting &MOM can be captured
SP 1.3 Manage Requirements Changes	change in product back log & CR for scope change
SP 1.4 Maintain Bidirectional Traceability of Requirements	product backlog ,a) Usage of Test& Review tool b) Add additional Sheet/column with Mapping to other Phases
SP 1.5 Ensure Alignment between Project Work and Requirements	update in Release plan/Release backlog, etc
Requirements Development	
SG 1 Develop Customer Requirements	
SP 1.1 Elicit Needs	User stories
SP 1.2 Transform Stakeholder needs into Customer	Business Requirements Document/user stories

Requirements	
SG 2 Develop Product Requirements	
SP 2.1 Establish Product and Product-Component Requirements	Software Requirements Specification/user stories categorized by module
SP 2.2 Allocate Product-Component Requirements	Software Requirements Specification/user stories categorized by module
SP 2.3 Identify Interface Requirements	User Stories related to Interface Requirements
SG 3 Analyze and Validate Requirements	
SP 3.1 Establish Operational Concepts and Scenarios	Use cases
SP 3.2 Establish a Definition of Required Functionality and Quality Attributes	Use cases
SP 3.3 Analyze Requirements	Use case review/Use Case prioritization
SP 3.4 Analyze Requirements to Achieve Balance	Use Case prioritization
SP 3.5 Validate Requirements	product backlog
Technical Solution	
SG 1 Select Product-Component Solutions	
SP 1.1 Develop Alternative Solutions and Selection Criteria	Minute of Architecture discussion/consolidated chits/ Alternative solutions/evaluation report/selection criteria
SP 1.2 Select Product-Component Solutions	Minute of Architecture discussion/consolidated chits/ Alternative solutions/evaluation report/selection criteria
SG 2 Develop the Design	
SP 2.1 Design the Product or Product Component	Product Architecture/Architecture drawn in the board- photo copies/ Consolidated chits /Minutes of Meeting on architecture discussion
SP 2.2 Establish a Technical Data Package	Use case, architecture documents, Unit tests
SP 2.3 Design Interfaces Using Criteria	Use case on Interfaces/architecture
SP 2.4 Perform Make or Buy Analysis	Minutes of design discussion/consolidated chits/

	evaluation/solutions bought to integrate
SG 3 Implement the Product Design	
SP 3.1 Implement the Design	Source code
SP 3.2 Develop Product Support Documentation	user manual/product manual
Product Integration	
SG 1 Prepare for Product Integration	
SP 1.1 Establish and Integration Strategy	Plan for System /integration test to expand the strategy
SP 1.2 Establish the Product Integration Environment	Build environment/Continuous integration details
SP 1.3 Establish Product Integration Procedures and Criteria	Build steps in wiki/notes
SG 2 Ensure Interface Compatibility	
SP 2.1 Review Interface Descriptions for Completeness	Integration test/Continuous build
SP 2.2 Manage Interfaces	Integration test/Continuous build/action items/standup MOM
SG 3 Assemble Product Components and Deliver the Product	
SP 3.1 Confirm Readiness of Product Components for Integration	Unit test/Continuous build
SP 3.2 Assemble Product Components	Continuous build/Build
SP 3.3 Evaluate Assembled Product Components	Sprint demo
SP 3.4 Package and Deliver the Product or Product Component	Release Details
Verification	
SG 1 Prepare for Verification	
SP 1.1 Select Work Products for Verification	Definition of Done details/User stories tasks
SP 1.2 Establish the Verification Environment	Code standards/XP method/checkpoints/tools
SP 1.3 Establish Verification Procedures and Criteria	Code standards/XP method/checkpoints & Definition of Done
SG 2 Perform Peer Reviews	

SP 2.1 Prepare for Peer Reviews	User story tasks/pair programming/automate code review
SP 2.2 Conduct Peer Reviews	Automated code review reports/Pair Programming correction in code/Refactoring
SP 2.3 Analyze Peer Review Data	Corrected code /automated code test re-run report/Refactoring
SG 3 Verify Selected Work Products	
SP 3.1 Perform Verification	Unit testing
SP 3.2 Analyze Verification Results and Identify Corrective Action	Defect Analysis activity to be made in addition to understand and prevent the Defects
Validation	
SG 1 Prepare for Validation	
SP 1.1 Select Products for Validation	System test plan/ Test approach for user stories & Release & product
SP 1.2 Establish the Validation Environment	Test Environment set up
SP 1.3 Establish Validation Procedures and Criteria	Test cases/Definition of Done
SG 2 Validate Product or Product Components	
SP 2.1 Perform Validation	Test Execution Results
SP 2.2 Analyze Validation Results	Defect Analysis activity to be made in addition to understand and prevent the Defects
Project Planning	
SG 1 Establish Estimates	
SP 1.1 Estimate the Scope of the Project	Scope of Work
SP 1.2 Establish Estimates of Work Product and Task Attributes	User story sizing (story point, fibinnoci series, etc)
SP 1.3 Define Project Life Cycle	Sprint cycles and release cycles
SP 1.4 Determine Estimates of Effort and Cost	User story sizing (story point, fibinnoci series, etc)
SG 2 Develop a Project Plan	
SP 2.1 Establish the Budget and Schedule	Release /sprint schedule , user stories by sprint
SP 2.2 Identify Project Risks	MOM of stand up meeting and Risk Log at product level proposed
SP 2.3 Plan for Data Management	Project plan/charter to be prepared
SP 2.4 Plan for Project	Capacity planning

Resources	
SP 2.5 Plan for Needed Knowledge and Skills	Scrum team guidelines & Skill identification
SP 2.6 Plan Stakeholder Involvement	Scrum team guidelines & Project charter/Meeting details
SP 2.7 Establish the Project Plan	Project plan/charter to be prepared
SG 3 Obtain Commitment to the Plan	
SP 3.1 Review Plans that Affect the Project	Revised Plan/charter
SP 3.2 Reconcile Work and Resource Levels	Revised Plan/charter
SP 3.3 Obtain Plan Commitment	Revised Plan/charter
Project Monitoring and Control	
SG 1 Monitor Project Against Plan	
SP 1.1 Monitor Project Planning Parameters	Velocity, Burn down charts, defects etc
SP 1.2 Monitor Commitments	Stand up Meeting, Running minutes of meeting/photos/snapshot/tool
SP 1.3 Monitor Project Risks	Stand up Meeting, Sprint planning & Risk log at release plan/product level, Running minutes of meeting/photos/snapshot/tool
SP 1.4 Monitor Data Management	Stand up Meeting, Running minutes of meeting/photos/snapshot/tool
SP 1.5 Monitor Stakeholder Involvement	Stand Up Meeting, Sprint Retrospective, sprint demo
SP 1.6 Conduct Progress Reviews	Stand up Meeting/sprint retrospective
SP 1.7 Conduct Milestone Reviews	Sprint retrospective/Steering Committee meeting, Use of wiki page/notes to capture MOM
SG 2 Manage Corrective Action to Closure	
SP 2.1 Analyze Issues	Stand Up Meeting, Sprint Retrospective & Issue log at Product/release level, Running minutes of meeting/photos/snapshot/tool (distributed teams)
SP 2.2 Take Corrective Action	Stand up Meeting, Running minutes of meeting/photos/snapshot/tool (distributed teams)

SP 2.3 Manage Corrective Action	Stand up Meeting, Running minutes of meeting/photos/snapshot/tool (distributed teams)
Risk Management	
SG 1 Prepare for Risk Management	
SP 1.1 Determine Risk Sources and Categories	To have broad classification of Risk (technical/process/environment, etc)
SP 1.2 Define Risk Parameters	Qualify risk with parameters at least by high/medium/low and use Product level/Release level Risk log & use in standup MOM
SP 1.3 Establish a Risk Management Strategy	Have a "Agile Guideline" document and update it
SG 2 Identify and Analyze Risks	
SP 2.1 Identify Risks	Stand up meeting/sprint planning & release planning, Qualify risk with parameters at least by high/medium/low and use Product level/Release level Risk log & use in standup MOM
SP 2.2 Evaluate Risks	Stand up meeting/sprint planning & release planning, Qualify risk with parameters at least by high/medium/low and use Product level/Release level Risk log & use in standup MOM
SG 3 Mitigate Risks	
SP 3.1 Develop Risk Mitigation Plans	Stand up meeting/sprint planning & release planning, Qualify risk with parameters at least by high/medium/low and use Product level/Release level Risk log & use in standup MOM
SP 3.2 Implement Risk Mitigation Plans	Stand up meeting/sprint planning & release planning, Update of status of closure in MOM or in Risk Log
Configuration Management	
SG 1 Establish Baselines	
SP 1.1 Identify Configuration Items	Prepare a Configuration plan/part of charter to include Configurable items
SP 1.2 Establish a Configuration Management System	Detail the repository/tools and change approval mechanism in Configuration plan
SP 1.3 Create or Release Baselines	Code- definition of done to include Baseline details & Continuous

	integration documents -list in wiki/notes
SG 2 Track and Control Changes	
SP 2.1 Track Change Requests	Change Requests as user stories/change request in tool/Update in product backlog
SP 2.2 Control Configuration Items	Change Requests as user stories/change request in tool/Update in product backlog/MOM
SG 3 Establish Integrity	
SP 3.1 Establish Configuration Management Records	snapshots from tools, CR status, continuous integration reports
SP 3.2 Perform Configuration Audits	Continuous integration reports, Sprint demo, release checks
Measurement and Analysis	
SG 1 Align Measurement and Analysis Activities	
SP 1.1 Establish Measurement Objectives	Velocity, defect, etc
SP 1.2 Specify Measures	Velocity, defect, etc
SP 1.3 Specify Data Collection and Storage Proc	Scrum tracking sheet can have guidance
SP 1.4 Specify Analysis Procedures	Burn down chart, velocity chart, etc
SG 2 Provide Measurement Results	
SP 2.1 Obtain Measurement Data	Burn down chart, velocity chart, etc
SP 2.2 Analyze Measurement Data	Burn down chart, velocity chart, etc
SP 2.3 Store Data and Results	Burn down chart, velocity chart, etc
SP 2.4 Communicate Results	Steering committee, sprint meeting, mails
Process and Product Quality Assurance	
SG 1 Objectively Evaluate Processes and Work Products	
SP 1.1 Objectively Evaluate Processes	SQA Audit on process shall be conducted. Any trained person can do the audit (SQA can be part of the team)
SP 1.2 Objectively Evaluate Work Products and Services	Work products reviewed for Process by any trained person. (SQA can be part of the team)
SG 2 Provide Objective Insight	

SP 2.1 Communicate and Ensure Resolution of NC Issues	Non compliance closure Report
SP 2.2 Establish Records	Non compliance closure Report
Integrated Project Management	
SG 1 Use the Project's Defined Process	
SP 1.1 Establish the Project's Defined Process	tailoring checklist/document (of organization process with project context)
SP 1.2 Use Organizational Process Assets for Planning Project Activities	Use of repository on defects/risks, etc
SP 1.3 Establish Project's work Environment	Project plan to have environment details
SP 1.4 Integrate Plans	Consolidate the Project plan, delivery schedule , product back log ,sprint backlog ,etc
SP 1.5 Manage the Project Using the Integrated Plans	Sprint planning, stand up Meeting
SP 1.6 Establish Teams	Scrum roles
SP 1.7 Contribute to the Organizational Process Assets	Sprint retrospective, MOM/wiki pages/notes -> to improve SCRUM application
SG 2 Coordinate and Collaborate with Relevant Stakeholders	
SP 2.1 Manage Stakeholder Involvement	Steering committee, stand up meeting
SP 2.2 Manage Dependencies	Steering committee, stand up meeting
SP 2.3 Resolve Coordination Issues	Steering committee, stand up meeting
Organizational Training	
SG 1 Establish an Organizational Training Capability	
SP 1.1 Establish the Strategic Training Needs	Linked training needs with business objectives (mostly annual Training plan /strategy document)
SP 1.2 Determine Which Training Needs Are the Responsibility of the Organization	Project level & Org level training - listed (in plan)
SP 1.3 Establish an Organizational Training Tactical Plan	Training delivery schedule, etc
SP 1.4 Establish Training	Training environment, trainer details

Capability	documented
SG 2 Provide Necessary Training	
SP 2.1 Deliver Training	Training delivery record (Invite/material/feedback/attendance)
SP 2.2 Establish Training Records	Training delivery record (Invite/material/feedback)
SP 2.3 Assess Training Effectiveness	Training feedback evaluation/360 feedback/performance check, etc
Organizational Process Focus	
SG 1 Determine Process-Improvement Opportunities	
SP 1.1 Establish Organizational Process Needs	Process Needs & details (mostly in Quality Manual)
SP 1.2 Appraise the Organization's Processes	Audit/appraise/review organization process
SP 1.3 Identify the Organization's Process Improvements	Improvement log (based on appraisals and from projects)
SG 2 Plan and Implement Process Actions	
SP 2.1 Establish Process Action Plans	Improvement Log (with CR/improvement and action plan)
SP 2.2 Implement Process Action Plans	Improvement Log status(with CR/improvement and action plan)
SG 3 Deploy Organizational Process Assets and Incorporate experiences	
SP 2.1 Deploy Organizational Process Assets	Deployment plan with status
SP 2.2 Deploy standard processes	Deployment plan with status
SP 2.3 Monitor the Implementation	Deployment plan with status
SP 2.4 Incorporate Experiences into the Organizational Process Assets	Updated Repositories (Estimation/risk/defects/samples, etc)
Organizational Process Definition	
SG 1 Establish Organizational Process Assets	Same as CMMI as they are Org. level practices
SP 1.1 Establish Standard Processes	Documented process Definitions
SP 1.2 Establish Life-Cycle Model Descriptions	SCRUM guideline

SP 1.3 Establish Tailoring Criteria and Guidelines	Tailoring Guideline (mostly by process) and Criteria (Co-located/distributed teams, etc)
SP 1.4 Establish the Organization's Measurement Repository	Metrics repository
SP 1.5 Establish the Organization's Process Asset Library	Repositories (Estimation/risk/defects/samples, etc)
SP 1.6 Establish work Environment Standards	Work Environment details (mostly in Quality manual)
SP 1.7 Establish rules and guidelines for teams	Teaming norms (mostly in Quality manual)
Decision Analysis and Resolution	
SG 1 Evaluate Alternatives	
SP 1.1 Establish Guidelines for Decision Analysis	Guideline (when to use, criteria, responsible, etc)
SP 1.2 Establish Evaluation Criteria	Criteria to evaluate decision(it will vary based on the context)
SP 1.3 Identify Alternative Solutions	Document alternate solution (separate DAR sheet used in many org.)
SP 1.4 Select Evaluation Methods	Evaluation techniques (Pugh matrix, cost benefit, weighted average, etc) (DAR sheet to have the method)
SP 1.5 Evaluate Alternatives	Valuation of each alternative solution (DAR sheet)
SP 1.6 Select Solutions	Final Solution (DAR sheet)

Alternate Practices:

In CMMI Model the goals are required component and practices are only expected components. However considering the practices are based on the Industry experience to great extent they are applicable in most of the context. Also they are neither tasks nor redundant practices, they are exclusive in nature. The practices can be interpreted for any context accordingly and in most of the context they are applicable. However very rarely organizations may have a context in which the Specific Goal is applicable however the practices are not really applicable. In that case, the organizations can document the alternate practices which they follow. The same can be shared with CMMI Institute.

A Sample case, when an organization's project is working using a complete lifecycle management tool with integrated resource planning software, in such case the Configuration Management Specific Goal 3 Establish Integrity, is met actually with existing environment which has all the configurable items in an well managed automated life cycle management tool (which include project plan, schedule, code, etc) and the tool also manages the versioning and without relevant information the tool doesn't allow you to save your work (such rules are part of the tool). In that case the Specific practice 3.1 and 3.2 may not be implemented but the Specific Goal is satisfied with the integrated life cycle tool environment and working within the tool. You can write the relevant practice and document as part of CMMI mapping with QMS and share with Appraisal team for evaluation. Again the case which we have taken here is for sample purpose and it can be interpreted and argued with more information.

REFERENCES

Websites:

- www.cmmiinstitute.com

- seir.sei.cmu.edu

- sei.cmu.edu

Articles, Whitepaper and Documents

- CMMI Model v1.3 Dev (TR)

- CMMI Model v1.3 Svc

- A Jumpstart Method for Business Goals and Project Objectives Supporting CMMI High Maturity - By Robert W. Stoddard

- High Maturity! How do we Know? – By Mike Konrad

- SCAMPI v1.3

- A Mini-Tutorial for Building CMMI Process Performance Models - Robert Stoddard, Kevin Schaaff, Rusty Young, and Dave Zubrow

- CMMI or Agile: why not embrace both! – Jeff Dalton, Hillel Glazer, David Anderson Michael D.Konrad and Sandra Shrum

REFERENCES

Websites:

- www.cmmiinstitute.com

- seir.sei.cmu.edu

- sei.cmu.edu

Articles, Whitepaper and Documents

- CMMI Model v1.3 Dev (TR)

- CMMI Model v1.3 Svc

- A Jumpstart Method for Business Goals and Project Objectives Supporting CMMI High Maturity - By Robert W. Stoddard

- High Maturity! How do we Know? – By Mike Konrad

- SCAMPI v1.3

- A Mini-Tutorial for Building CMMI Process Performance Models - Robert Stoddard, Kevin Schaaff, Rusty Young, and Dave Zubrow

- CMMI or Agile: why not embrace both! – Jeff Dalton, Hillel Glazer, David Anderson Michael D.Konrad and Sandra Shrum

A Sample case, when an organization's project is working using a complete lifecycle management tool with integrated resource planning software, in such case the Configuration Management Specific Goal 3 Establish Integrity, is met actually with existing environment which has all the configurable items in an well managed automated life cycle management tool (which include project plan, schedule, code, etc) and the tool also manages the versioning and without relevant information the tool doesn't allow you to save your work (such rules are part of the tool). In that case the Specific practice 3.1 and 3.2 may not be implemented but the Specific Goal is satisfied with the integrated life cycle tool environment and working within the tool. You can write the relevant practice and document as part of CMMI mapping with QMS and share with Appraisal team for evaluation. Again the case which we have taken here is for sample purpose and it can be interpreted and argued with more information.

www.ingramcontent.com/pod-product-compliance
Lightning Source LLC
LaVergne TN
LVHW022323060326
832902LV00020B/3643